architecture

Ulf Meyer / Alain Linster

LX architecture – in the heart of europe contemporary architecture in luxembourg

Edited by
Fondation de l'Architecture et de l'Ingénierie, Luxembourg

introduction 01

14	**LX architecture** christian bauer
16	**architecture at the heart of europe** ulf meyer
20	**constructions of a watchful society** ulf jonak

contents

28 culture

MUDAM, Luxembourg **28** Musée National d'Histoire et d'Art, Luxembourg **34** Casino Luxembourg, Forum d'art contemporain, Luxembourg **38** beaumontpublic gallery, Luxembourg **42** Philharmonic Hall, Luxembourg **46** New National Library, Luxembourg **52** Stade Albert Kongs, Hesperange **54** Centre National de l'Audiovisuel & Centre Culturel Régional de Dudelange, Dudelange **58** Cultural Centre Maison Thorn, Niederanven **66** Rockhal II, Esch-sur-Alzette **70** Chapel, Oetrange **74**

78 work and trade

Production Hall/Offices, Leudelange **78** Cement Works, Esch-sur-Alzette **82** Production Hall with Administrative Wing, Echternach **86** Jean Schmit Engineering, Luxembourg **90** Office Block, Luxembourg **94** Provisional Conference Centre, Luxembourg **96** Workshops of the Administration des Ponts et Chaussées, Bertrange **100** Conversion of an Industrial Building, Niederanven **104** Laccolith, Cloche d'Or **108** General Secretariat of the European Parliament, Extension and Alterations to the Konrad Adenauer Complex, Luxembourg **112** European Court of Justice, Luxembourg **116** Extension for the European Court of Auditors, Luxembourg **122** Conference Centre, Luxembourg **128** Heights Offices, Luxembourg **134** Rehab Centre "Rehazenter," Luxembourg **138** SES, Betzdorf **146** Soteg, Esch-sur-Alzette **150**

156 banks

Annex for a Bank, Luxembourg **156** Commerzbank Luxembourg (CISAL), Luxembourg **162** IKB International, Luxembourg **166** European Investment Bank II, Luxembourg **170** Zentralbank II, Luxembourg **174** Banque Populaire du Luxembourg, Luxembourg **178**

182 education

Pre- and Primary School, Remerschen **182** Foyer scolaire and École précoce-préscolaire, Hamm **186** Pre- and Primary School, Eich-Mühlenbach **190** School in Born, Mompach **194** Extension of a Primary School, Howald **198** Sports Hall for the École primaire Dellheicht, Esch-sur-Alzette **202** Extension to the Rue du Verger Primary School, Luxembourg **206** Pre- and Primary School, Bettendorf **210**

02

214 **urban development**

Master Plan for Porte de Hollerich, Luxembourg **214**   Redesign of the Centre of Hesperange **218**   Ex-Industrial Site Esch-Belval, Competition, Esch-sur-Alzette **222**   Station District, Luxembourg **228**

234 **residential**

Reconstruction of a Former Dairy, Bettembourg **234**   Social Housing, Bettembourg **238**   Maison Zambon, Dudelange **242**   Detached House, Bridel **246**   Conversion of the Site of the Former Tile Factory Cerabati, Mertert-Wasserbillig **250**   Maison Schneider-Peter, Peppange **252**   Youth Hostel, Echternach **256**   Residential Estate, Bertrange **260**   Residential Housing, Rumelange **264**   Villa, Luxembourg **266**   Renovation of an Old Town Quarter, Luxembourg **270**   Villa De Meyer-Fasbender, Villa Freising, Luxembourg **274**   Moko House, Schuttrange **278**   Avalon, Luxembourg-Kirchberg **282**

286 **gardens and parks**

Garden of the Banque de Luxembourg, Luxembourg **286**   Parc Jacquinot, Bettembourg **290**

292 **pavilions**

Arcelor Pavilion, Esch-sur-Alzette **292**   Economie Pavilion, Esch-sur-Alzette **294**   Skip Pavilion, Esch-sur-Alzette **296**   Pavilion, Heinerscheid; Light Bar, Luxembourg **298**

300 **infrastructure**

Terminal A at Luxembourg Airport **300**   Block-Type Thermal Power Station, Luxembourg-Kirchberg **306**   Radar Tower, Luxembourg-Findel **312**   Reservoir, Hivange **314**   Route du Nord, Viaduc de Lorentzweiler **316**   Reservoir / Technical Service and Fire Department, Leudelange **318**

322 **patrimony**

Emile Mayrisch Monument, Esch-sur-Alzette **322**   The Red Bridge, Luxembourg **324**

reflection

03

334　**constructive** emmanuel jean petit

appendix

04

345	**biographies**
347	**credits**

01

introduction

14 **LX architecture** christian bauer
16 **architecture at the heart of europe** ulf meyer
20 **constructions of a watchful society**
ulf jonak

LX architecture

President of the Fondation de l'Architecture et de l'Ingénierie Luxembourg
Christian Bauer

LX Architecture. Not to be confused with XL, as in size terms we are more of an S, in the sense of small. Maybe SL Architecture would have been an alternative? No, the label "small luxury" does not suit us either. All the same, here is a book on architecture in Luxembourg. Not that its publication is simply down to Ieoh Ming Pei's museum and Christian de Portzamparc's Philharmonic Hall. Certainly, the reputation of those architects had an influence, with their finished buildings providing the experts with a few surprises. However, in recent years international competitions have attracted a great number of European architects and landscape planners to Luxembourg. The Fonds du Kirchberg, the Luxembourg planning authorities, the Agora Belval, the Fonds Belval, the municipality of Esch and the City of Luxembourg, all have articulated their requirements and aspirations giving birth to an urban development and architectural initiative likely to exercise long-term influence. Both private individuals and local developers have begun to adopt the trend, ensuring that this new architectural stimulus does not remain limited to a few beacon projects.

A quick delve into Luxembourg history reveals that despite the country's limited size and the provinciality of its people time and again the occasional foreign planner or architect has imposed a visible mark. Édouard François André, the French landscape architect, contributed to the remodelling of the Plateau Bourbon and is famous for having designed the city park. The German urban planner Hermann Josef Stübben significantly influenced the city's urban development at the dawn of the twentieth century. Alain Bourbonnais, the French architect, designed the capital's main theatre. His compatriot Pierre Vago was responsible for remodelling the city centre in the 1960s, with his colleague Robert Joly, another Frenchman, the main author of the 1990s update to the urban landscape. In the early 1980s, the English architect, Denys Lasdun, designed the first buildings for the European Investment Bank on the Kirchberg plateau.

Sustained economic growth in the 1990s and Luxembourg's expanding role as the seat of many European institutions has resulted in numerous imprints on the built environment. At the latest with the development of the Kirchberg plateau, internationalisation of the Grand-Duchy's architecture took off rapidly. Under the influence of Jochem Jourdan, an urban planner from Frankfurt, the numerous foreign banks as clients and the Fonds de Kirchberg as strategic authority, architectural quality finally rediscovered its place as a general criterion. The architects Gottfried Böhm, Richard Meier and Atelier 5 were the first to impose their unmistakable stamp on the plateau. The qualitative impetus set in motion by the imported architects provided a major boost to the local architectural scene. At the same time, it must not be forgotten that the Banque de Luxembourg already broke ranks in the late 1980s, rebelling against the architectural mediocrity of the Boulevard Royal. Harnessing the architecture of Arquitectonica, Jean-Michel Wilmotte's interior design and the landscape planning of Jacques Wirtz this became the location for a monument with both contextual and contemporary features at the very heart of the capital. Following the stimulus generated by the status of Capital of Culture in 1995, the Luxembourg State began to invest increasingly in buildings housing art and culture. In winning the services of Ieoh Ming Pei and Christian de Portzamparc leading world-class architects were engaged to fulfil those ambitions.

In the early 1990s a few idealistic architects founded the Fondation de l'Architecture et de l'Ingénierie. All had studied architecture in one of the neighbouring countries and wanted to compensate for the absence of a Luxembourg school of architecture. They began to hold conferences to which they invited architects from all corners of the world, and in this way introduced many an international stimulus to the domestic scene. In addition, this sharpened the awareness of local clients and public authorities for the significance of architecture. The local planning partnership of Hermann & Valentiny, already a recognised name abroad, finally became an accepted figure at home. European rules further encouraged greater openness and self-confidence in Luxembourg architecture. Foreign and Luxembourg practitioners participated in competitions on equal terms. With satisfying results. Even if a jury was headed by an expert from abroad, the domestic scene was neither deceived nor ignored. Instead, the local scene has been enriched, strengthening its abilities to meet future challenges.

A start has been made. Within a short while architectural travel guides will appear with Luxembourg as their sole focus.

architecture at the heart of europe

Ulf Meyer

From a sleepy mini-State to the Washington of a new world power

Luxembourg is booming. Since the 1950s this small country has enjoyed sensational – almost unparalleled – growth in its political, economic and cultural importance. After World War II, its situation and role as buffer between France and Germany (in historical terms neither easy nor free from risk) proved to be a major advantage. In the course of the reconciliation process between its two large neighbours, traditionally each other's enemy, Luxembourg assumed the role of mediator. As the European Union grew to become one of the world's most important trading and political alliances the small mediaeval town of narrow streets transformed itself from the seat of government of a mini-State shattered by the demise of its steel industry into the Washington of newly discovered world power. However, in urban planning and architectural terms design vision sadly always lagged behind political function. Although the new district planned for the Kirchberg plateau after World War II certainly was an urban development project with utopian feel, its plans extending so far into the future that even today they remain nowhere near fulfilled, what Luxembourg always lacked was the creative determination which characterised Brasilia, Canberra or other purpose-built capitals. Even today that deficit continues to be painfully felt. Not even the best architecture can paper over those weaknesses in urban design.
It is a testament to the skillfulness of Luxembourg's political strategy that even following EU enlargement to a community of 27 Member States this small country's role has not been seriously called into question. For architecture this favourable geopolitical situation was a good starting point and opportunity which in recent years Luxembourg has seized with rapidly increasing success. Whilst in the 1980s it was the banking industry which almost overnight raised Luxembourg to the status of one of the EU's leading financial centres – today, the country is the world's seventh largest financial centre – the large and prestigious cultural projects which followed such as the MUDAM, the Philharmonic Hall and the National Library have allowed an image of Luxembourg as a cultural centre to flourish. Hardly had this awakening national self-confidence taken hold, as a consequence of EU enlargement yet a third wave of growth was unleashed on the city, heralding a new construction boom.

Luxembourg City is one of the most heavily globalised small towns in the world. The share of the population accounted for by foreigners – more than 40 percent in rural areas – is easily outstripped in the capital, two-thirds of whose residents originate abroad. More than 120,000 frontier workers commute from the surrounding regions of neighbouring countries to the land of economic miracles; the European institutions situated in Luxembourg are responsible alone for the employment of some 7,500 non-nationals.

From dirty steel to pristine banknotes

Luxembourg's rise to a city with an importance felt across the entire continent began in 1952 on its designation as the headquarters of the European Coal and Steel Community (ECSC). Five years later Luxembourg was one of the founding members of the European Economic Community (EEC). Whilst the coal and steel industry has long ceased to be at the heart of Luxembourg's economy, financial services have taken its place. Favoured by an advantageous legal framework and attractive rates of tax, financial services currently generate 45 percent of the country's gross domestic product, account for 12 percent of all jobs and provide the State with over 40 percent of tax revenues.
As the seat of the European Court of Justice, the European Court of Auditors, the European Investment Bank and the Secretariat of the European Parliament, Luxembourg can call itself home to a unique concentration of key European institutions.

GDP per head has reached a figure of 65,900 US dollars and at this level more than twice exceeds the EU average. More than 86 percent of Luxembourg citizens work in the modern service sector. In no other country of the European Union has the crisis in manufacturing accelerated the trend towards a service economy as sharply as in Luxembourg. Today, alone the number of banks registered in Luxembourg has reached some 177, not to mention the many investment funds, holding companies and insurance and reinsurance entities.

Pei, Perrault, Portzamparc – Is there such a thing as Luxembourg architecture?

Architecture in Luxembourg has an international flavour. This phenomenon applies just as equally to clients and practitioners as it does to their intellectual father figures. All Luxembourg architects have trained abroad, for the simple reason that even today the Grand-Duchy continues to lack a professional training scheme for architects. For that reason, on their return to Luxembourg, graduates of foreign universities have imported influences and experiences acquired abroad. The numerous foreign clients, strongly influenced by the architecture of their home countries, provide an additional foreign dimension. These factors impart the Luxembourg scene with a rarely found diversity.

In the 1980s projects by the banks were particularly responsible for bringing internationalism to the fore. Mainly designed by famous international architects, these buildings sprang rapidly like mushrooms from the local earth. Gottfried Böhm built on behalf of Deutsche Bank, the adjoining plots became home to Richard Meier's plans for Hypobank and Arquitectonica's design for Banque de Luxembourg, meanwhile Denys Lasdun created new premises for the European Investment Bank and later the Swiss architectural concrete experts from Atelier 5 did the same for the HypoVereinsbank headquarters.

The European Court of Justice building, designed in 1973 by Jean-Paul Conzemius, illustrated the architectural affinity shared by banks and the EU's bureaucratic institutions. The generally well-appointed structures to which both the institutions of capital and bureaucracy have given birth form certainly an interesting collection for the architectural zoo and reflect not least the architectural zeitgeist of recent decades. However, the steady accumulation of buildings by famous architects on the Kirchberg plateau sadly has not resulted – even today – in the emergence of a neighbourhood desirable for living. Time and again the rule was proven that a good individual piece of modern architecture often entails an anti-social approach to urban design. Even if prominent public buildings followed in the shape of Roger Tallibert's "Olympic" swimming pool and later with Ieoh Ming Pei's well-known modern art museum and Christian de Portzamparc's neighbouring Philharmonic Hall, amongst experts the Kirchberg plateau is considered a prime example of a missed opportunity to reshape Luxembourg City – not to mention the absence of a convincing model for the urban and architectural appearance of the EU bureaucracy.

A similarly major boost to new construction had been first experienced by Luxembourg almost a century earlier, in the years following 1867, a development made possible by the removal of the historical fortifications choking the city's core. On that occasion, the plateau opposite the city centre was the site for a new district centred on the railway station, planned in architectural and urban design terms in keeping with the historicist ideals of the period as a lively residential and commercial area, whose features remain compelling even today. That period, too, saw recourse to the services of two foreign experts in landscape and urban design: Édouard André from France and Josef Stübben from Germany. Whilst André was responsible for designing the wonderful romantic parks of Luxembourg City, Stübben drew up plans in 1901 for the city's extension on the Bourbon Plateau, accessed via wide new bridges spanning the steep gorges.

Modernist architecture arrived in Luxembourg only after a delay. It did not achieve popularity in Luxembourg until 1929, the year of the exhibition "Wie wohnen?" ("How should we live?"). The Grand-Duchesse Charlotte maternity hospital, designed by Otto Bartning, was inaugurated in the year in which in Germany the Nazis had already sounded the death-knell on modernism.

The development of the plateau on the Kirchberg began in turn with a bridge. Following the construction of the well-known and elegant Pont Rouge, the first architectural fixed point arrived in the form of the new municipal theatre by Bourbonnais (1964), joined a year later by the office block on Place de l'Europe by the architects Gaston Witry and Michel Mousel – in those days a solitary and abandoned anchor in an archetypal car oriented model city of the modern age.

Bridges, banks and bureaucrats

Only following the turning point of the late 1960s ushering in the postmodern era did the world in Luxembourg begin to change. Although in 1964 the task of redesigning the old town went to the modernist Pierre Vago, history's reappearance in architectural debates was irrevocable. Luxembourg soil sprouted two of the most prominent postmodernist thinkers, the brothers Robert and Léon Krier. When in 1976 Rob Krier built the family residence "Dickes House", a building reduced to cube-like form, the new era in Luxembourg had its first icon.

In the postmodern era, new importance was attached to living in the city centre, in particular, the old town district. Not only around the Marché aux Poissons (fishmarket) were old buildings restored and new apartments, restaurants and shops constructed, but also improvements in cultural terms were made to the city's core. Conny Lentz's Luxembourg City Museum soon found itself in the company of a new high-class neighbour, the Museum of National History and Art by Christian Bauer. Nowadays, demolition of old buildings would not awaken dreams of a better future, but furious protest.

The postmodern approach – thinking in terms of as-built plans, streets, blocks and squares – is set to arrive finally on the Kirchberg, too, with numerous enhancement and consolidation measures planned. Even if in architectural circles postmodernism has been long since considered démodée, its authority in the realm of urban planning – and in that sphere only – lies beyond question.

constructions of a watchful society

Ulf Jonak

A small country. Crossed in no time at all. Plenty are found entering. Clouds sailing in from the west, transporting a few breaths of sea air, perhaps. Convoys of cars sporting registration plates from Trier and Bitburg enter from the east, lay siege to the filling stations and empty the pumps of their fuel – so much more reasonably priced in this country.

It has always been this way: always someone uninvited is crossing the frontier. Spaniards, Frenchmen, Austrians, Germans all occupied the country before once again releasing their grip. Only the country's heart, its capital city, stood unshakable in the midst of a territory overrun, its defences strengthened by Vauban to become the most secure bastion in Europe, with only Gibraltar coming close in comparison. From afar, Luxembourg, the city, appears mighty. Its seemingly endless casemate batteries, some 24 kilometres (15 miles) in total, have long since ceased to serve their original function. Nowadays, they are visited in the course of a Sunday outing, displaying a pride in the invincibility enjoyed in bygone eras. Accordingly, from the outside, today, the bastion appears to represent the over-protective amour-plating of a society in search of cohesion. When the frontiers to the outside world are rotting away identity is not easy to preserve.

The "financial bastion" is under attack from firing positions beyond the frontier, allegedly a hindrance in the fight against money-laundering and similar types of financial crime. In the course of European unification radical changes in this area appear unavoidable, even though the desire exists to see the strongroom even more securely fastened. Curling up like a hedgehog certainly enjoys a tradition in this small country which encourages all too invitingly that response. Revealing in their details are the turreted oriel windows found everywhere in towns and villages, endowing the homes of the lower middle-class with the character of a mini-fortress. An architectural psychologist investigating "architecture and insecurity" would find plenty of raw material here to hand.

Thus, is there such a thing as a Luxembourg style of architecture? An architecture built around security and defensiveness? If so, it exhibits gestures of a more playful and experimental nature. For a time the Krier brothers caused a furore in the world. But even that highly succinct oft-cited family home "Dickes House" (1974) in Bridel by Rob Krier, with a street elevation penetrated only by embrasure-like openings, withdrawn within itself as if the ultimate example of Luxembourg stability, appears merely more in the style of a clay building from the High Atlas. The rendered roof edging once inspired by maghrebian tradition and damaged subsequently as a result of European rain, is protected today with a metal cover. This small constructional detail is highly characteristic of the uncompromising stance taken by young architects, but at the same time also typifies the desire (summoned from a foreign holiday – only to be given inadequate consideration) pursued both by the individual and the many in their search for originality and characterises, moreover, the creative over-zealousness with which they all too often overlook not only the constraints of their own circumstances but also the existence of traditions tried and tested. The qualities of the region are considered – as is so often the case – worthless in their country of origin.

Retreat into the private sphere is an element of human nature observed throughout the world and cannot be regarded as a behaviour typical only to Luxembourg. Nonetheless, the visitor here is struck by a particularly introverted mood. Despite the open-mindedness practised in public, distance is maintained in private affairs. Neighbourhoods and villages appear more empty than in neighbouring countries. Whilst the Dutch like to treat exterior walls as a surface for projection and the French generally also make

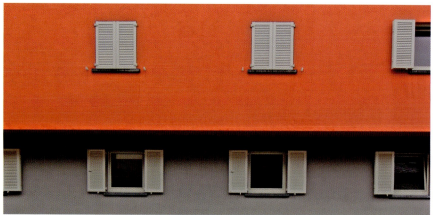

generous use of glass, the walls here in Luxembourg appear more solid, and although slit, cleft, ruptured and pierced, access or insight remains denied.

The gesture conveyed by Aristide Gambucchi's award-winning detached house in Mondercange with its shear wall in Pompeian red is reminiscent of that portrayed by the residential building in Dudelange developed from the same architectural perspective by the offices of m3. Both are endowed with narrow observation slits or embrasure-like window openings facing the street. Both display the red-coloured rendering elements of their façades as shields against a potential attack. This architectural language is not unknown. Internationally, it is widespread. Only it appears more strongly than elsewhere to be indebted here to a latent yearning for security. A desire which finds itself accommodated, too, in the contemporary tendency to break down façades in a series of successively positioned layers.

Unsurprisingly, at a certain point the stranger begins to feel as if he is an intruder. He appears to be met constantly by built forms which are obstructed, covered, reserved or martial in appearance. On the capital's Kirchberg the block heat and power station by Paul Bretz is reminiscent of the monumental power station projects of the futurist Sant'Elia, surpassing even that individual's radical prime symbolism. The building appears as if an addition to a mighty defence system. Close to the ARBED blast furnace complex, already a threatening looking unit in itself, lies Hermann & Valentiny's laboratory and office building in Esch-Schifflange constructed from grey, solid, sculptural concrete as if a bunker on the Atlantic Wall. Under the heading of attempts at seclusion, introversion and isolation it is possible to include also the minimalistic buildings of a certain Christian Bauer.

Even the buildings of the 1920s and 1930s inspired by the "international style" appear more robust here than elsewhere. The pasta factory in Dudelange, sympathetically converted to residential units by Hermann & Valentiny in 1996, is in accordance with the fashion of the inter-war period amply divided by horizontal lines and mouldings, in such quantity as if the aim were to resist with bars or transoms the all too expansive continuity of of glass exhibited by contemporary architecture. Harnessing the same techniques Hubert Schumacher's Chapelle du Christ-Roi (1931) demonstrates a inviting openness, shielded at the same time through the use of wall channels and solid horizontals in the style of glazing bars. Strong bands, as if fixing a belt around each construction to ensure cohesion, can be seen in the villa architecture of the period, too. Quite conceivably, everywhere in central Europe buildings constructed around 1930 reflect a general sense of insecurity. However, the impression cannot be denied that – as a result of its previous painful experiences – Luxembourg was the most forceful in deploying the symbolism of watchfulness.

Thus, is there such a thing as a Luxembourg style of architecture? Subject to a few mild doubts, the question may be answered in the affirmative. Although appearing today predominantly in a playful context, the characteristic national gestures of security and defensiveness clearly exist. But, as if national frontiers had evaporated, here, too, architecture ever increasingly acquires a more international hue. And, from time to time, more colourful, too. Here, Léon Glodt's buildings in Bridel, decorated in bold parrot-like colours, display a recalcitrant show of impudence in the face of stable and defiant common sense.

As if attracted by the riches of the financial centre, the skies above Luxembourg are increasingly snowing foreign architects. Although each brings with them their own language, the ordering of their design alphabet pays homage to the local spirit. Ieoh Ming Pei uses existing fortification structures to hold in place the crystalline glass form of his Musée d'Art Moderne Grand-Duc Jean (MUDAM).

Gottfried Böhm built for Deutsche Bank on the Kirchberg, playfully incorporating a castle-like turret motif. Nearby, Richard Meier steeled his Hypolux Bank with oversized shields. Denys Lasdun's European Investment Bank with its extended horizontal decks from the distance resembles two marauding aircraft carriers. The Banque de Luxembourg – designed by Arquitectonica – in the city centre is staged as nothing short of an aggressive scene, in which stone and glass elements collide.

Whether a bank, museum or theatre, a large public building functions always as a magnet. These are at the centre of momentary forces of attraction and, accordingly, must not create all too great an impression of a barrier. In most such cases weighing openness against security becomes an acrobatic feat. The Centre des Arts Pluriels in Ettelbruck, an organically shaped solid object with glass-walled inserts, illustrates this balancing act. An even more elegant display of this artistic achievement is to be found on the Kirchberg. Christian de Portzamparc's Philharmonic Hall gives the impression of a forest of columns bathed in light. Yet, it appears to curl up as a hedgehog, its vertical spikes raised. Hence, an attraction and, at the same time, an object to be approached with care. In addition, inside the building, in the large auditorium, towers of spectator balconies edge the audience space as if security guards hailing from a land of giants.

The measures needed to secure a remote location are less blatant, albeit no more subtle. In that vein, a development of apartment buildings, a neo classical style white acropolis, on the Limpertsberg has appeared, the work of the Spanish architect Ricardo Bofill. However, the destination to which the observer is transported in his imagination is neither Spain nor Greece let alone Luxembourg, but a gated community where the upper classes celebrate luxury. Resting on a cliff-edge, exclusively positioned as if home to the gods, its residents are seemingly secure from attack.

Thus, is there such a thing as a Luxembourg style of architecture? In the Birkhäuser *Architectural Guide Netherlands Belgium Luxembourg 20th Century* the authors write: "Das Großherzogtum Luxemburg ist in dieser Hinsicht ein weitgehend unerschlossenes Land mit einem offenbar geringeren Interesse an der Architektur als Identität stiftendem Faktor" ("In this regard, the Grand Duchy of Luxembourg is an undeveloped country for the most part, apparently with slight interest in architecture as a factor contributing to identity."). That view is likely to be shared by anyone searching for a conscious, local form of architectural symbolism. The matter is rather different, if one credits the subconscious as imbued with archetypal forces forcing their way to the surface. Those who appreciate how to read such signs, discover in the body of Luxembourg architecture a wealth of references to underlying fixations, to history and local traditions.

This small country: plenty of architectural food for thought.

02

architecture in luxembourg

- 28 **culture**
- 78 **work and trade**
- 156 **banks**
- 182 **education**
- 214 **urban development**
- 234 **residential**
- 286 **gardens and parks**
- 292 **pavilions**
- 300 **infrastructure**
- 322 **patrimony**

03 04

orient/occident

culture

MUDAM, Luxembourg

Architect
Ieoh Ming Pei,
Pei Cobb Freed & Partners
New York,
Georges Reuter
Architectes Luxembourg,
2006

The capital of the prosperous Duchy of Luxembourg is shedding its image as a dry city of banking and bureaucracy, and becoming known as a city of culture. Its ambitious cultural infrastructure program began in the 1980s under the government of Jacques Santer. The first highlight of the overhaul is the new Musée d'Art Moderne, designed by Chinese-American architect Ieoh Ming Pei, who was directly commissioned by Santer to create the new museum.

Known as the MUDAM, the museum is located on the Kirchberg plateau above the city. It stands on the ramparts of what was once the eighteenth-century arrow-shaped Fort Thüngen. Pei, who is based in New York, says "Luxembourg was and still is today a crossroads, the place where Germany meets the rest of Europe … The fortress was the natural symbol, the physical symbol of the country … And within the rock they had a castle, and within the city there's a network of tunnels so the residents could move around and defend themselves. That was of great interest to me. I was curious to know how Luxembourg remained an independent country – that's why I accepted the commission."

This 88 million euro museum in Luxembourg is to be Pei's last work in Europe. It has also been his most drawn-out. Completion was delayed a number of times because, against the wishes of the architect, the historical fort was not linked to the art museum, necessitating a relocation of the main entrance to the other side. There were also years of wrangling over the expensive, honey-coloured Burgundy limestone cladding the Museum walls inside and out and which is crucial for the mood of Pei's spaces. But all that will be forgotten when the building – whose formalistic outward appearance takes a lot of getting used to – proves that it is a fitting home for art. The introverted form of the neighbouring fort is reflected in the new building: Pei has designed an enclosed central space like that found in traditional Chinese architecture. The northern façade, behind which the exhibition galleries are located, has only minimal openings, while the glass southern façades provide views of the old city. Sculptural stairways tempt the visitor in the foyer to mount to the upper floors. Because the art collection was still being built up when the commission for the museum was given, the architect was not able to design rooms specifically for particular exhibits. And yet, the building is in no way neutral. The architecture does not dominate the art; rather, it offers it a framework which in turn regards itself as a work of sculpture.

The movement of the visitor takes on a meaning of its own in this building. The elegant staircases make taking a turn through the collection a matter of carefree lightness. From the Grand Hall, the 33 metre high centre of the building topped by a square glass tower, one's eye is drawn to the "Dräi Eechelen" – the three acorns of Fort Thüngen. Daylight enters the first-floor exhibition rooms via shed roofs not visible from the outside. The lower floor with its subdued light is dedicated to the new media. Oak parquet, gypsum-paneled walls, and exposed concrete reflecting the grain of the fir wood into which it was poured, give the rooms a pleasant, contemplative feel.

⌃ Natural stone and concrete mark the opening areas

❭ Exhibition halls

⌄ **The geometry of the new construction follows the ruins of the fort**

The visitors to the museum take an architectural promenade. The play of light and shadow enlivens the atriums

pure

culture

Musée National d'Histoire et d'Art, Luxembourg

Architect
Christian Bauer & Associés Architectes, 2002

Christian Bauer's sharply-cut block of natural stone, which dominates the Fish Market, rubs many up the wrong way. The entrance façade has been called a "Wailing Wall" by the locals. The glazed ground floor, looking like it was cut out with a scalpel, only allows you to guess at the entrance. Once you do step inside, you find yourself in a well-ordered foyer. This precise new building appears like an appendix to the historical building and has 4.600 square metres of exhibition space. That volume was only possible because the building that links them, with its extensive ramps, serves as a *promenade architecturale* like those created by Le Corbusier in the 1920s. The ramps lead up as well as down into the subterranean depths. Bauer knows how to increase tension, and not only to accept the gaps and spaces between the old and the new, but also to articulate them as unexpectedly fortuitous encounters.

On the outside the long, low cube is almost hermetically sealed in limestone; only the side facing onto the square opens at its base, with a narrow glass band. This is where the entrance to the museum is. The foyer stretches out behind it. Anyone who visits the museum must first ascend a few steps from the downward-sloping street to the flat plane of the plaza. Involuntarily, you stop walking somewhere in the middle of it and look around: no, the space is still agreeably empty; there are, as yet, no flowers in tubs or benches to upset the composition. Reassured, you enter the foyer, surrounded by genteel restraint of form and material. A few steps further on, the encounter with the interior of the museum becomes a sudden sensation – behind the foyer, the space opens up wide to the heavens through the glass roof above. And all at once, you understand the concept hidden within the building.

The museum is composed of three parts. A historical town house forms its backbone; the new museum in front of it is the body, and in between is the stairwell with its glass roof, forming a powerful joint. Above this central stage – formally an homage to Modernist architecture – the old and the new buildings are linked by walkways.

The old building, which was already in use as a museum, today holds the collection of paintings while the new building is dedicated to archaeology.

Cleverly, the architects have not spread out the new museum horizontally but vertically. Surfaces piled up on top of one another appear to grow like metaphors out of the depths and the darkness of early history towards the light of the modern period. Below street level, vaulted cellars from 1580 hewn out of the living sandstone were integrated into the building. The bedrock on which Luxembourg is built and which forms the museum's foundations has become the building's universal motif, giving a rustic air to the seemingly rough and unrefined ambience of the archaeological exhibition. Particularly clever is the use of light in the new building, which elegantly combines light from natural and artificial sources. A narrow chink of light is visible on the entrance side facing the square. It forms the edge of the façade, mirroring the line of the band of light running around the outside of the square. At the same time, this glass gap takes daylight right down to the lowest level, where archaeological artifacts are exhibited in the twilight. Natural light and spotlights set into the ceiling work very well together here.

The very stimulating transitions between the old and the new make the museum a place of sensory experiences: you enjoy the well-balanced contrast of colours and materials in the old and new buildings, you look through the windows of the old building into the courtyard and with your fingertips, you feel the roughness and coolness of the massive stone. The project turned the carefully-restored historical façade of the old museum into an element of the interior. A soft, inviting light shines out of the contoured windows in this façade, and you are glad to follow it. The newly arranged collection is presented in an ever-changing series of introverted cabinets, large and small rooms. A mild, almost smoky light, pastel colours on the walls, and the warm wood tones of the parquet floor ensure a contemplative mood.

⌄ The longitudinal section shows
the true dimension of the museum

⟩ Old and new come together in the
opening room

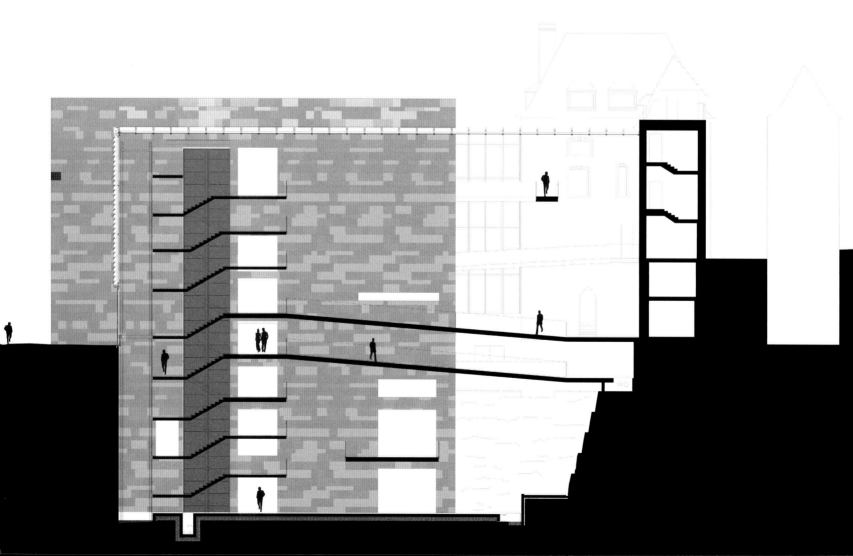

cube

culture

Casino Luxembourg, Forum d'art contemporain

Concept
Urs Raussmüller, 1995

The city's old Casino was turned into an exhibition space for contemporary art in 1995, when Luxembourg was a European City of Culture. The principle of the White Cube – prominent since the 1960s – dominated the renovations, which were carried out by Urs Raussmüller. The twelve exhibition modules he installed for the presentation of modern sculpture have been put to the test in recent years by a number of artists.

For the exhibition Un bel été in 1997, the largest of these exhibition modules on the first floor of the old Luxembourg Casino was torn down to make way for a symbolic work for the artistic exploration of the reception of the work itself by the public. To this end, the art collectors Annick and Anton Herbert made available the work Public space/Two audiences by Dan Graham (1976). This work is considered one of the icons of its tradition in contemporary art, whose object is the relationship of the work of art as a thing that must fit with the building it is displayed in – and the visitor to the exhibition himself.

Public space/Two audiences is an enclosed space with two different entrances that is divided inside by a wall of soundproof glass. On one side, the artist placed a mirror in which members of the public could see themselves; this reflection was however also the only image to be observed in a white room.

Simone Decker employed another method for her exhibition To be expected. She cut up entire panels from an exhibition module on the ground floor, and reordered them in a kind of playful architecture in the White Cube opposite. In this way, the principle of the original exhibition by Urs Raussmüller was sculpturally and architecturally deconstructed and alienated from its original form. Other artists also chose to undermine the non-spaces or transitional spaces in the casino: for instance, Sam Samore and Nedko Solakov, whose text-graffiti spread out over niches, backdrops, and the hidden transitions of the hybrid architecture – thereby opening up exhibition spaces that Raussmüller never thought of in his original concept.

↖ The cubes are at a noble distance from the façade

▲ Deconstructed module as an installation object

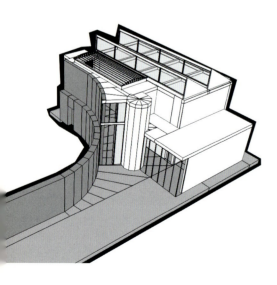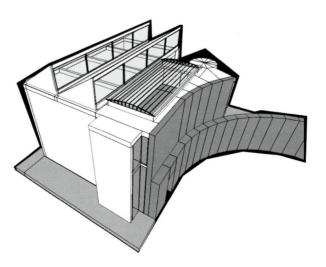

l'art pour l'art

beaumontpublic gallery, Luxembourg

Architect
Moreno Architecture & Associés,
Gubbini & Linster Architectes, 2001

culture

Museums are traditional places for exhibitions. By contrast, the open street is hard to comprehend as a place for art, because it provides a freedom that allows us to discover the art of tomorrow. Between these two extremes is the private gallery – a display window for experimental forms which are nevertheless already recognized by collectors. Part of their makeup is a special space to attract attention from outside.

The beaumontpublic gallery, however, is a gallery that in no way corresponds with this high-visibility criterion. It is not located in the centre of the city, but in a peripheral residential area – and on top of that, it is at the back of a garden. That means that, along with her professional reputation among the artists, the owner, Martine Schneider, needs a fat address book full of collectors, and an unshakeable faith in word-of-mouth advertising to attract art lovers. Typologically, the gallery brings to mind a building in a royal park, *la folie*, as pavilions for music and contemplation in the Baroque period were called. The description certainly matches the gallery's location in the garden newly designed by landscape architect Marc Schoellen, and in the discovery of contemporary art which is the goal of every new exhibition. The location itself was once a cold storage place for a brewery. Based on the storage shed, the gallery has a structural lightness; the building could be dismantled simply and easily. A rough layer of rendering gives the whole thing substance. Nor does the interior subscribe to the idea of transience. On the contrary – even the curtain rails with their carefully-finished ends have the precision you would find in a museum. Is this gallery therefore a collage? Its composite appearance and a certain roughness – the stairs up to the library, the lights in the shape of industrial shingles above the main room, the wooden slats as a reminder of the storage shed – are all in stark contrast to the finely-finished interior with its aseptic white walls. Owner Martine Schneider has made the architects Marc Gubbini and Stefano Moreno line up against each other. She needs the strictness of the one just as much as the imagination of the other for the outer structure and for the special use of light. The main exhibition room is reserved for large-format pieces, while the side gallery serves for the showing of smaller formats.

⌄ Art in space

⌄ **Daylight washes the white walls** ⌄ **Impressions of space**

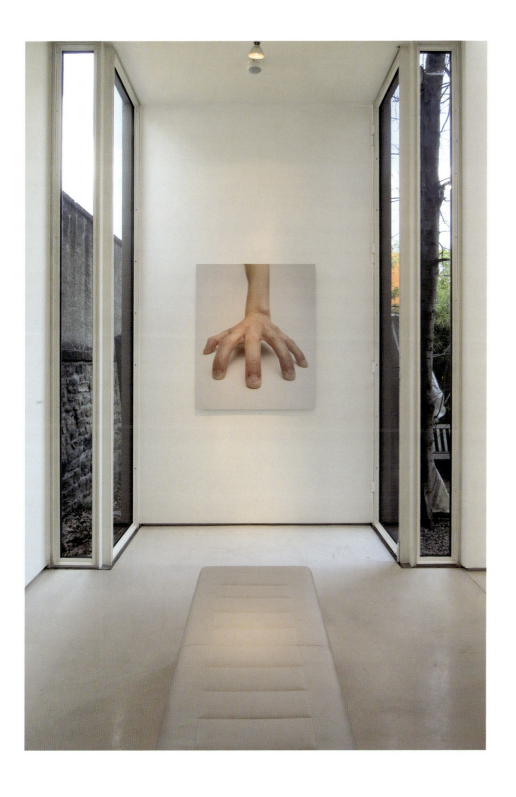

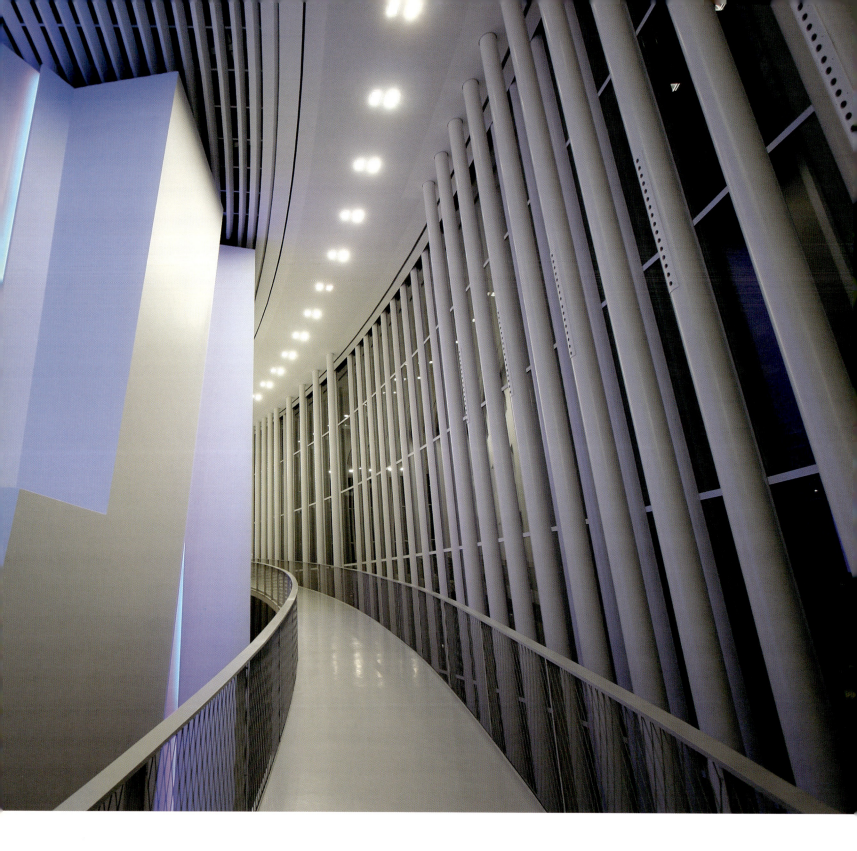

space for initiation

Philharmonic Hall, Luxembourg

Architect
Christian de Portzamparc, 2005

Contact architect
Christian Bauer & Associés Architectes

culture

Unifying the processes of seeing and hearing in a synaesthetic experience must surely be the aim of every architect designing buildings for music. The realm of music, by its very nature, usually has to be separated from the profane outside world.
In his blueprint for the new Luxembourg Philharmonic Hall, Christian de Portzamparc created "a space for initiation," which like a filter of light introduces those entering to the world of music. Exactly 827 white steel supports surround the building's inner concert hall. In order to separate the Philharmonic Hall from the uniformity of office blocks in the Quartier Européen around it, the architect constructed a freestanding shell of up to four parallel rows of supports around it. The space for music in the middle stands inside it like a building within a building. Luxembourg has not in the past been recognized as a great place of culture; it was overshadowed by its reputation as the home of banks and EU bureaucracy. Now the Place de l'Europe is being transformed into a cultural district. The new Philharmonic Hall is the first concert hall in the Grand Duchy. It is located on Avenue John F. Kennedy, halfway between the city centre and the airport. Ieoh Ming Pei's museum of modern art has opened nearby. Luxembourg City could well have the most ambitious cultural building program of all the European capitals – particularly considering that it has a population of just 80,000.
In the surrounding, dazzlingly bright foyer of the 107-million-euro concert hall light also enters from above. A flat ramp winds its way through the 18-metre-high foyer to eight "towers" containing the boxes, which are placed around the Grand Auditorium. The spaces between them are painted in bright colours and are illuminated at night by neon lights. This trick immerses the scenery of seeing and being seen – the essence of every theater foyer – in iridescent light. The tower-like boxes appear almost as buildings in their own right, standing around a piazza. The main concert hall is a classic shoebox auditorium done in black. The only colour accent is in the pearwood paneling on the boxes and the frame of the organ by Berlin master organ-builder Karl Schuke. Unlike other new concert halls in Europe – Rem Koolhaas' Casa da Musica in Porto for instance – Portzamparc's conception of space is conservative but stands back to let the music take pride of place. It almost seems as if Portzamparc followed the ideas of musical theorist Paul Marsop, who as early as 1903 called on the builders of a concert hall to make a "space, which is composed solely for the purpose of allowing music to develop unhindered all its mood-creating miraculous forces." (*Der Musiksaal der Zukunft*)
The concert hall, now home to the Orchestre Philharmonique du Luxembourg, has proven its qualities. The acoustics are "dangerously good," say the musicians – adding that every note can be heard clearly. The Chinese-French acoustics specialist Xu Ya Ying, who has worked with Portzamparc on projects such as the Cité de la Musique in Paris-La Villette, designed an ornamental acoustic ceiling here with mobile panels that allow the formation of different acoustic spaces. The shell-shaped chamber music hall is located below the auditorium and was named Salle de Concerts Grande-Duchesse Joséphine-Charlotte, after the late Duchess.
Portzamparc, who himself plays piano and flute, has earned his reputation as the "composer among architects."

⌃ Light and shadows in harmonious austerity

⌃ Seeing and being seen in the surrounding foyer

⌃ Boxes form the side boundary of the auditorium

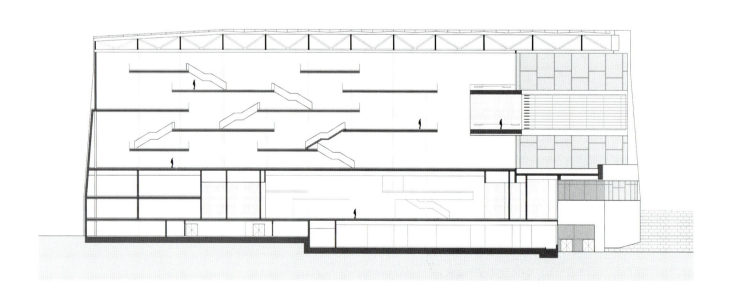

vista

New National Library, Luxembourg

Architect
Bolles+Wilson
GmbH & Co. KG, 2004

culture

The Bolles+Wilson firm of architects from Münster took first place in the competition for a design for a new National Library on the Kirchberg plateau. This new building provides some 50,000 square metres of space for the library's more than 400,000 books and 480 seats for reading.

The design is meant to accommodate a future collection of three million documents. To this end, the current 1960s Robert Schuman building is to be redesigned and integrated.

The spreading roof, with its set-back text illuminated from behind, is like a signal in the direction of the old town. The eastern façade, however, provides a restrained framework for the triangular Place de l'Europe. The National Library is a new interpretation of the eight-storey prefabricated grid of the Schuman building. Instead of the stone corners of the old office block, there is now a spectacular, five-storey, showcase-like reading room, which enters into a dialogue between the library and the city. The roof gives the reading room the necessary shade. Two "reading boxes" are suspended like aquariums in the folded glass surface. The second courtyard of the original building is now home to the heart of the archives, whose central position ensures optimal access from the offices on the northern side and from the reading galleries on the southern side of the building.

The base of the building which raises this world of books to the level of the treetops and gives it views of the city, takes up the topography of the area. It contains the foyer, the restaurant, and the conference rooms. The entrance rooms link the Place de l'Europe and the park landscape below.

All the façades including the roof are encompassed in printed glass. The dark, rich blue-grey beneath it shimmers through this membrane.

old and new

Stade Albert Kongs, Hesperange

Architect
Bruck + Weckerle Architekten, 2007

culture

In 2001, the municipality of Hesperange decided to upgrade the Stade Albert Kongs on the Itzig plateau. The old changing rooms, built in the 1970s, were no longer up to modern requirements. The architects Bruck + Weckerle integrated the existing building into the new one. In line with the soccer federation's requirements, the architects developed two separate entrances to divide the movement of spectators from that of the players. Through the new building, the clubhouse is now in even closer relationship to the playing field. The new building stretches from the level of the half-way line to the edge of the pitch. A concrete base was built around the existing building and the new one, with stepped concrete seating facing the pitch all along its length. A separate entrance was constructed for the players at the interface of the new and old buildings, as well as a covered area for the new and the old changing areas. The public areas include the Club Buvette with seating for forty people, as well as a kitchen with a grill. The players' area in the new building is made up of two sets of changing rooms with showers, two changing areas for referees, and a storage room. The development here was not planned as a long corridor – rather as a bright space with light from above. In the renovated old building there are two further cloakrooms; on the upper floor are the executive committee meeting room and the VIP room. The shape of the building was "smoothed" to ease the flow of people. The side facing the street is slightly dented, so as to guide the fans towards the ticket box. This bend in the façade creates a covered area on the side facing the pitch. The players, too, are guided towards the field by the funnel-like shape.

The entire building is clad in robust wood, linking the old and the new buildings and striking a sharp contrast with the surrounding residential area. Folding shutters make it possible to seal off the entire building. Inside, exposed concrete was used. Rainwater is collected in an underground tank, and is used for the shoe-cleaning equipment and to water the pitch.

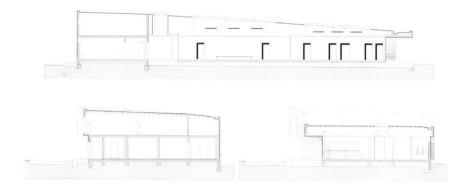

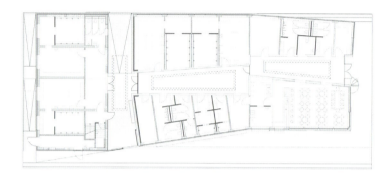

⌄ A wide variety of wood colours reveal themselves towards the playing field

⌃ Wood also marks the street façade

⌃ On the inside: exposed concrete

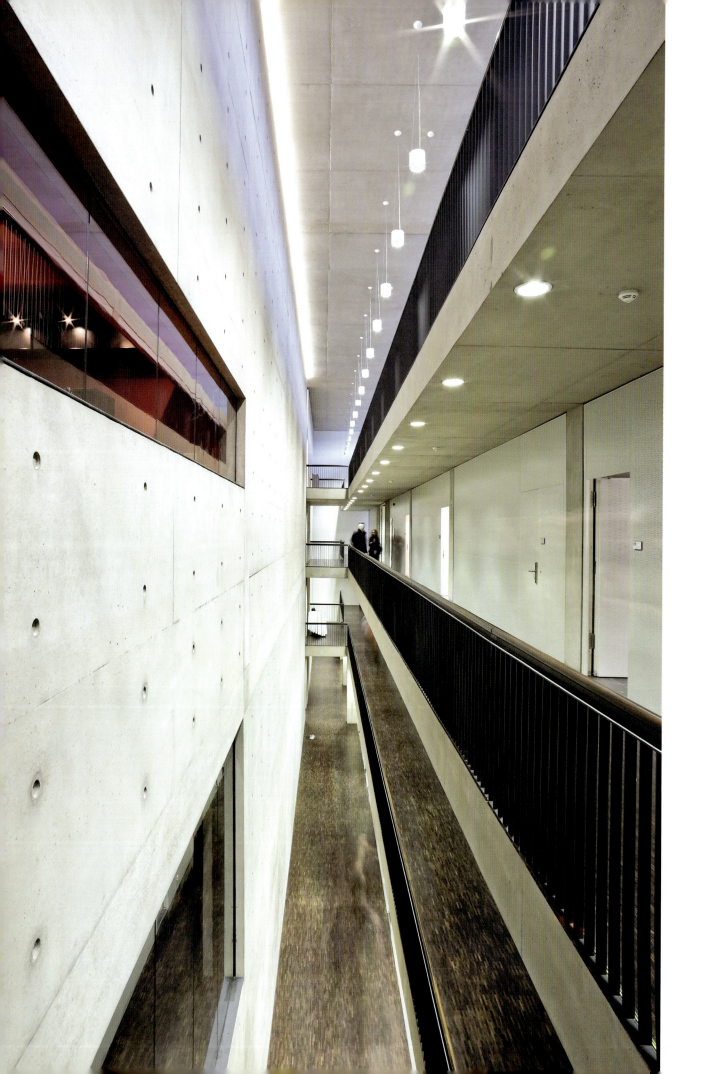

action

Centre National de l'Audiovisuel & Centre Culturel Régional de Dudelange, Dudelange

Architect
Paul Bretz Architectes, 2007

culture

The „Centre National de l'Audiovisuel (CNA) & Centre Culturel Régional de Dudelange (CCRD)" are a joint project between the town of Dudelange and the state of Luxembourg, and is to be built on the site of a former smelting works. The cultural institutions currently located around the town are to find a joint home in the new building. The smelter's former water tower is a part of the culture project and after its renovation is to house the exhibition "The Bitter Years." The location is easily reached from the town: on the northern side, a green belt along a stream provides a footpath to the nearby town centre and the railway station.

The CNA produces, processes, and archives film and sound recordings as well as and photo documents. It also lends out its material and organizes exhibitions. A media library, an exhibition room and a sales room are planned for the public areas. In the professional area, there will be a film studio, a sound studio, a small cinema, offices and laboratories, as well as equipment rooms. The lower floor will hold the archive. The CCRD will be home to a music school, rehearsal rooms for musical groups, and studios with conference rooms. The auditorium for 480 people, a cinema, and a cafeteria will be shared by the CNA and CCRD.

Despite the complexity of the project, the architects have been able to design a building of great clarity. The four-storey, square building is divided into a grid of 7.5 metre by 7.5 metre squares. The main entrance is a covered area which serves both as a forecourt and a connecting link, raised as it is from street level. The foyer provides good orientation for the visitor, who can reach the atrium and the rooms for events from here. At the end of the foyer are the CNA and the music school. They are reached via long, open galleries. The airy spaces create horizontal and vertical visual relationships throughout the entire building. From the outside the exposed concrete gives the building a monolithic appearance, while the space inside presents itself as a series of "exposed concrete boxes," which are freely arranged and can been seen in impressive size from the atriums. Long slits provide the open-air spaces and the atriums with natural light. Depending on the weather and the season, very different moods are created.

❰ Cultural institution with the rough charm of the former industrial grounds

↑ The strict cubic grid continues in the rear area as well

˄ Contrasts of colour and material in the interior   ˃ View and section

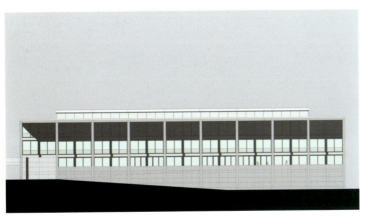
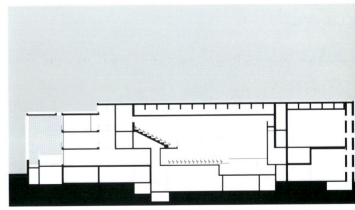

old alongside new

Cultural Centre Maison Thorn, Niederanven

Architect
Steinmetz De Meyer architectes urbanistes, 2006

culture

Maison Thorn, in a park with big trees, was enlarged and converted into a cultural centre with space for one hundred people. The architects intervened only slightly in the original building, so as to protect it as far as possible and to define areas for new activities. The existing rooms are used as offices for the tourist information service and as artists' studios. Cultural events take place in a new pavilion nearby. The new building with its light framework of steel, wood, and glass, appears to hover above the ground. Its architecture clearly differentiates itself from that of the old building. Old and new are easily recognizable, comprehensible, and reinforce each other.

Between the house and the new building are stages for open-air events. The Maison Thorn remains massive and relatively closed; the new building, however, is open to receptions, parties, cabaret, exhibitions, concerts, and colloquies. The gallery combines an entrance, cloakroom, and reception area along with a bar. The big hall is made of the typical local wood and gives an impression of warmth. To the south, there is a wooden terrace with a view of the park. The pavilion is suited to a number of different events; its large openings provide a view of the park and of the Maison Thorn. The gables are protected from the sun by plants – a metal structure with fine stainless steel cables supports the climbing plants.

⌃ The new construction makes the building into an „L" shape

⌄ The sections show the flexibility of the gallery rooms

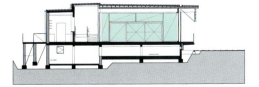 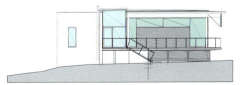

rock it

culture

**Rockhal II,
Esch-sur-Alzette**

Architect
Atelier d'Architecture
Beng, 2005

On the heels of their "Box in the Box" project in the neighbouring Blower House the architects have now designed a concert and rehearsals hall, a space available to musicians "wishing to develop their talents". The spacious hall can hold up to 5,400 people and is fitted out for concerts featuring both big stars and lesser-known performers. A more intimate hall for smaller concerts and, "studies and experiments in light, sound and movement" can hold up to 800. The Centre de Resource contains rehearsal rooms, recording and dance studios, a library and a mediatheque.

The architects were faced with the task of creating a striking building against an industrial backdrop that included two blast furnaces. The large hall, more than twenty metres in height, and its smaller, more modest cousin are both cast in rough, black concrete. Hovering over the concrete cubes is the Centre de Recherche with its red façade and large glass apertures offering breathtaking views across to the neighbouring blast furnaces and industrial plant. Black and red – the colours of rock.

⌃ Two halls of different sizes are used for concerts and rehearsals

quiet

Chapel, Oetrange

Architect
Tatiana Fabeck Architecte,
2005

culture

The chapel is situated in the centre of Oetrange beside a church and a cemetery. The paucity of materials employed, the subtle use natural and artificial light and the building's formal simplicity are conducive to the calm and contemplative atmosphere of a funeral service.
The location itself determined the materials used in the construction of the chapel. The old walls of the cemetery were preserved and restored. An inner structure of concrete is encased in stone. Large, steel sliding doors allow the entire interior space to be opened up.

⌃ Form and light create a calm space

› Simple materials allow for contemplation

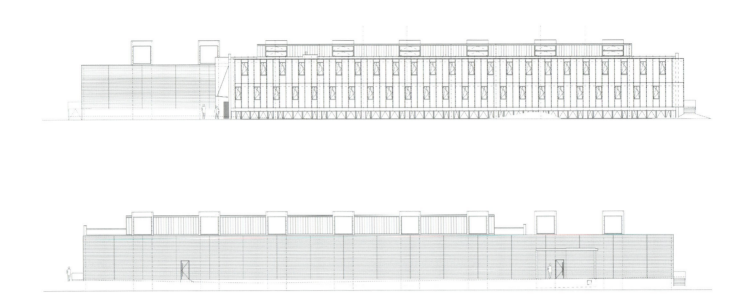

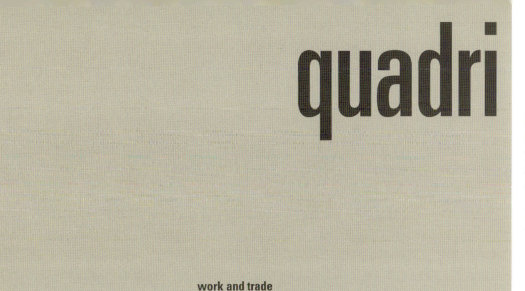

work and trade

Production Hall / Offices, Leudelange

Architect
Steinmetz De Meyer architectes urbanistes, 2001

Commercial buildings are usually only about function, but this design is also about the quality of life for those working inside.
The offices in the north and the hall in the south are linked by an internal "street" open on two levels which let the daylight shine in. This street is a pleasant place to be, and it promotes meetings and communication between the people working here. On the eastern side, the street ends in an entry hall which has the air of a piazza. The cafeteria is a place for the staff to gather, where they have the best view of the impressive rotary presses that can be seen through a large glass wall. These machines are the reason for the building's existence, and have therefore been made the focus of its spatial composition.

The hall, without any internal supports, is a wooden construction of 45 by 80 metres. Thanks to their transparent cladding of polycarbonate panels, the box girders over the entire breadth of the hall serve as skylights. Each section of roof is suspended between the box girders. The exposed concrete structure of the office building communicates with the floor surface, the made-to-order furniture, and the partitions made of wood and glass. The technical equipment and the acoustic elements are a visible part of the interior decoration.

❯ **Main entrance**

⌣ **Stairwell**

‹ Offices and processing hall

⌄ Cafeteria

‹ Print Shop

concrete

work and trade

**Cement Works,
Esch-sur-Alzette**

Architect
Hermann & Valentiny und
Partner, 2000

This new laboratory and administration building is located next to the cement works in an industrial area belonging to Groupe Ciments. The architects planned "a building that has the strength to encompass the spatial randomness of the existing buildings, incorporating them into one space and to communicate a special corporate identity to the company using architecture and design."

The staggered arrangement of the storeys is an adaptation to the topography of the land. The factory floor at the lower level opens up onto the factory grounds toward the south and pushes north, with laboratories and equipment rooms below the main level. This level is also home to the social rooms and the canteen; above that is the administration, with generously-proportioned access ways and airy spaces which link the levels optically and provide views of the premises.

Inside, unconcealed elements such as exposed concrete and brickwork, polished composite floors, high-grade timber surfaces, and bright colours dominate. The façades on the south side appear as a closed, inclined concrete wall, which has its counterpart in the slightly-inclined roof of the laboratories, made of the same material. The all-glass façade, oriented towards the north, provides optimal conditions for those working behind it.

The linear, 55 metre long building has two storeys on the side facing the street. It forms the new, representative face for a heterogeneous ensemble of silos, conveyor belts, and production halls; and at the same time, it turns its back on them. Glass offices two storeys high open up towards the street on the north side, while the foundations of the building, with the canteen, laboratories, and washrooms, are dug into the landscape on the sloping southern side. This part of the building has few windows and looks rather like a helmet with the visor pulled down; horizontal blinds in front of the rows of windows protect the workers from being watched from outside and from the heat of the sun. Prefabricated concrete elements form the walls, ceilings, and roofs of the new building.

In order to build rationally, Hermann & Valentiny divided up the shell of the building into a grid of 2.5 metre squares, and gave it a uniform cross-section along its entire length. The access area is the communicative core and design showpiece – indirect light, oak parquet, and perfectly-finished details in the interior decoration counteract the rigid modularity of the building's shell. Natural light enters only from above; floodlights provide a dramatic note for the sloping back wall. A few linear elements such as the row of windows over the office doors, and the flat, tube-like industrial radiators stress the length of the building. The balustrades on the stairs are made of asymmetrical sheet steel: one balustrade is bent along the handrail, thereby protecting the lighting integrated inside it – and the other handrail is flat. As the client did not demand reversible office structures, three dividing walls are supporting walls of reinforced concrete.

Rough exposed concrete, galvanized steel, clearly-structured wood and glass façades, and wooden surfaces dominate the picture, which fits harmoniously with its stony, industrial surroundings.

⌣ The new construction takes its place beside the large plants of the cement factory

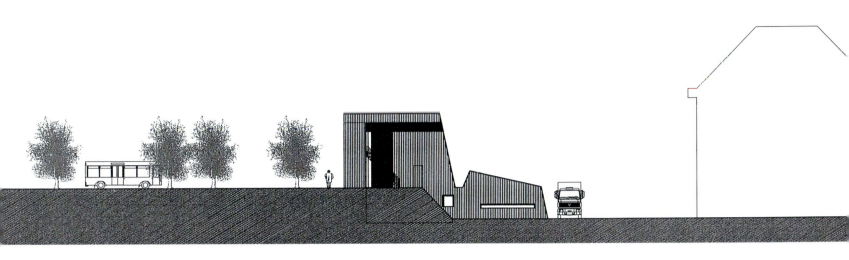

⌄ The building begins to glow
magically during the evening

far sight

Production Hall with Administrative Wing, Echternach

Architect
Christian Bauer & Associés Architectes, 2001

work and trade

Minimalist architecture is a phenomenon from the end phase of civilization. Minimalization is less a matter of functionality than one of uncompromising aesthetics. It is a symbol of mathematical precision the like of which we only find at the microscopic level.

The block of the production hall lies among the meadows of the hilly landscape around Echternach as if it had fallen from above. A shelf reaches up towards it from the ground, a pedestal made of rough stones, packed in gabions, archaic in its appearance, a bucolic wall motif, perhaps a reminiscence on the vineyards not too far away. Above it, the shining steel panels rise, looking like walls polished all in one piece, shaped into a cube. There are no secondary shadows, no projections, no deep recesses, only a few necessary slots. Even the edges of the large gates appear to have been carved out of the façade with a knife. Anyone approaching this metal object via the meandering road will first see a few parasitic foreign bodies: a hot-dip galvanized steel table, pushed against the wall as if docked there – the entrance to the office wing. On the north-eastern corner, a surprise awaits the visitor: one side is completely made of glass, looking like an over-dimensioned wide-screen television. There, the office wing opens up, a quiet area without drama. As in real television, the firm name and logo can be seen in the top left-hand corner.

The architect's creative imagination is revealed in the intelligent and convincing arrangement of the individual elements within the geometric shape. The maxim is not insertion, but contradiction against the existing. Christian Bauer loves stark contrasts – the archaic against the technical, the artificial against the natural. Rebellion as an attitude for design.

⌃ Floor plan

⌄ Cube on the field: industry meets nature

⌄ Daylight floods the common rooms

rust red

work and trade

Engineering Bureau
Jean Schmit Engineering, Luxembourg

Architect
Christian Bauer & Associés Architectes, 2002

The façade of the building is rust-red. Depending on the angle of the sun, it can be dull and tend towards brown, or it can be radiant and warm, almost orange. The colour and material are actually not typical for the Belair residential district. But this is not one of the 1950s homes that are the usual in this well-to-do quarter; this is a studio. The address 13, Avenue Gaston Diderich was first a carpenter's workshop, then home to a small producer of cooling systems, and then a printing works. And today, following substantial renovations between 2000 and 2002, it is the office of an engineering firm.

The new complex is divided into four parts. On the ground floor of a former apartment house are the firm's conference rooms. A long passage like a narrow corridor leads past them to the offices themselves. The main building consists of the old former studio, as well as a new block and a courtyard that links the two. The new block is connected to the building located on the street, so that the four structural elements form a whole. In this newly constructed linking element, there is a small open garage next to the passage. The garage houses an intelligent elevator system for an optimal use of the space.

The impression that the architects and the owners have taken care over environmental aspects is strengthened when one enters the offices. While the outer façade of the main building is resolutely modern, behind the entrance, the fine old structure of the studio becomes clear: a framework of steel girders and concrete is sparingly filled out with red brick to create windows that allow in the greatest possible amount of light. During the renovations, the only change to the historical structure of the façade was to put in new windows. The courtyard, which forms the link between the former studio and the new block, was given a glass roof. The concrete floors on the upper storeys were covered with parquet.

Building regulations prevented the construction of a new edifice, so the architect exploited the qualities of the existing one. The basic idea was to completely clean up the disfigured and often reworked original building, and to uncover its structure. The intention of the architect – to give the completed project its own strong identity – involves the minimalist design principle of working from the existing structure and to merely reinforce or correct what is there. Supports were merely lengthened, levels taken beyond their original plan. A row of bricks was added to bring the rhythm of the windows back into harmony; and the only materials used were those already employed in the building's past. But for the execution of their plans, the architects had to use the latest technologies: thermal insulation and double glazing were put in, the building received a layer of insulation on the outside, and the roofs were given a topping of living plants. The use of Corten steel on the façade is another extension of the ideas used inside: steel is the shared context inside and out. Inside the building, it is seen in the form of girders; outside, it forms an element in the façade.

❮ The new construction is situated deep in the property

❮⌃ The interior lives from the contrast between old and new

↑ The evening illumination shows the composition of the building structure

city building block

Office Block, Luxembourg

Architect
Arlette Schneiders
Architectes, 2004

work and trade

The client wanted a building that would be both modern and timeless, and that would still make its presence and its independent elegance felt. Unfortunately, two old villas on the site had to be torn down to make way for the project.

The district is characterized by its small plots of land; the challenge was to prevent the office building from appearing like an enormous block. The orthogonal subdivision that cuts across the Boulevard Grande-Duchesse Charlotte in a curve frames the project: a central block stands, not parallel to the street, but at right angles to the neighbouring buildings. The architect designed a shining stone monolith, which would give the building a strong presence, particularly at night. The central block is meant to feel massive but light at the same time. This monolith stands to the east, facing Place Winston Churchill, like a hinge that joins the orthogonal and rounded elements together.

To help the new building blend in with the surrounding cityscape, the architect used the colours of the surrounding buildings: yellow sandstone and beige-white rendered façades. The sunshields on the central block were made of sand-coloured terracotta, and for the holed façades, Spanish limestone is used. The staircase and access way that reaches from the entrance to the offices is behind the blinds that offer a good view of the Place Winston Churchill.

meeting-place

work and trade

Provisional Conference Centre, Luxembourg

Architect
Atelier d'Architecture & de Design Jim Clemes, 2003

The European Union delegation building is a temporary edifice with a timber frame and is located at the trade fair grounds. It is used only three months a year.

The three-storey building is more than fifty metres long. Its upper floors contain offices for the national delegations, while the ground floor houses offices for the European Commission, the general secretariat of the Council, and the country holding the EU presidency, offices for the observer states, and a conference room.

The temporary conference infrastructure for the Council of Ministers is set up in the exhibition halls 4 and 5 and has its own entrance. The modules for each delegation – foyer, secretariat, conference room, minister's office – are identical and can be reached from the corridor. The supporting structure consists of a gluelam framework and a stairwell of reinforced concrete and a steel-frame emergency escape stairwell on the gable end. The floor ceilings are made of prefabricated elements consisting of ceiling beams with waferboard panels and mineral rock wool insulation. Carpets, veneer plywood, and suspended ceilings of perforated metal coffering characterize the interiors. The façade consists of a non-bearing cleat construction made of individual elements with a cladding of black rubber. Their attachment at various points to the construction underneath gives the building the appearance of a giant pillowcase.

All the details reveal the temporary character of the building

public works

Modernization of the Workshops of the Administration des Ponts et Chaussées, Bertrange

Architect
Bruck + Weckerle Architekten, 2007

work and trade

The central workshops of the Administration des Ponts et Chaussées were constructed on seven hectares of land in Bertrange's industrial zone. The grounds, characterized by undefined left-over spaces, were rather unstructured, and the position of the buildings in relation to one another and to the street was fairly random. New workshops, a salt storage facility, garages for trucks, as well as depots, offices, and meeting rooms are planned for the location. The architects chose a linear, additive arrangement for the buildings, placing them in rows according to function and circulation. Linear buildings shield the grounds from the outside and protect the adjacent residential areas. In the middle row are the buildings with special functions, such as the salt storage facility, a police station and a park. Two broad, internal service roads provide access to the area, which is divided into three zones with different functions. Parking spaces are located off the premises.

The minimalist industrial architecture is driven by the demands of function. Floor spaces and eaves heights are matched to the length of the relevant vehicles and the space required for the equipment. Extra storeys in the form of galleries can be put into the buildings. While the edifices located on the outer rim have closed outer façades, their inner sides open up with projecting roofs. The façades are made of specially-developed aluminium profiles reminiscent of a guardrail. These six metre long and 30 centimetre high elements are mounted at irregular angles to one another, thereby creating a weave-like surface that patterns over the joins in the building. The closeness of the façade communicates calmness, stops people from looking in, and is interrupted only by systematically-distributed, narrow windows. The garages and workshops have glass gates leading onto the service roads; this makes orientation easier.

In the large halls, the constructive elements are also the visible surfaces. The horizontal elements of the steel for the outer walls can be seen alternating with the vertical structure of the Reglit walls and the fluted structure of the trapezoid metal plates that serve as supports for the skin of the roof. In the offices and social rooms there are softer materials, such as rubber, covering the walls and floors, as well as warmer colours.

⌃ Various colours mark the different functions

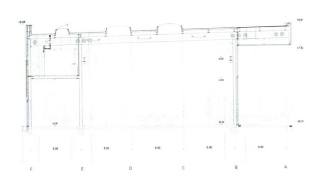

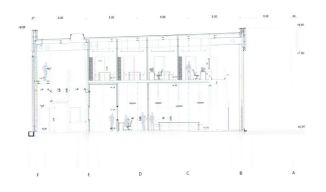

⌃ The gates open up mysteriously

⌄ From far away, the building
  presents itself as if covered by
  a giant chequer-board pattern

new team

work and trade

Conversion of an Industrial Building, Niederanven

Architect
Steinmetz De Meyer architectes urbanistes; in collaboration with Njoy by Nathalie Jacoby et Jill Streitz, 2006

A large industrial building – originally a carpentry workshop – was converted into an office block for eighty people to work in. The challenge for the planners was to create work spaces with an identity in what was a rather faceless area.

The façade is made up of two different prefabricated parts: window frames, consisting of one large double window with a clear pane for looking out of, and an opaque part for ventilation.

Vertical blinds and shelves form modules in the façade of the self-supporting wooden building. The façades are clad with Douglas fir wood. A courtyard was placed in the middle of the old production hall. The cafeteria, the secretariat for the company management, the assembly hall, and the rooms for the designers are grouped around it on two levels. Individual offices, group workrooms for engineers and technicians, as well as small conference areas were placed along the outer walls.

⌄ **The direction of light makes orientation easier**

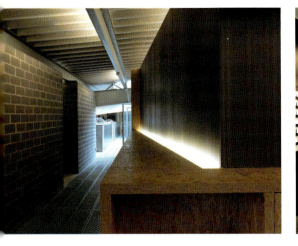

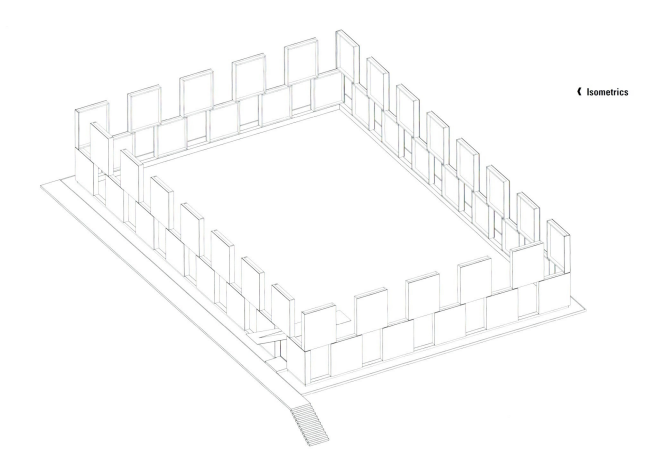

❮ **Isometrics**

⌄ The built-in furniture follows the spatial concept

⟩ Floor plan

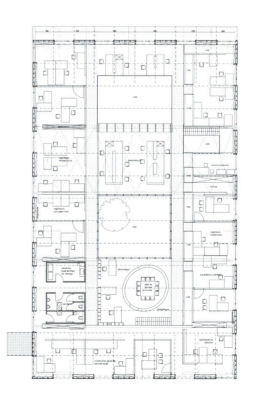

understatement

Laccolith Office Complex, Cloche d'Or, Luxembourg

Architect
Paczowski et Fritsch
Architectes, 2002

work and trade

Luxembourg shines. The new cathedrals of cash blaze brightly, and the outgrowths of commerce are opening their brightly-coloured buds even in the most remote suburban wastelands. One of them is the administration building called *Laccolith* in the easily-accessible district of La Cloche d'Or. *Laccolith* – the very name melts in the mouth. The building's attraction lies in the cool understatement of steel and glass, and the inescapable magic of "great forms under the light" (Le Corbusier).

This system of "great forms" is clearly structured within *Laccolith*. Two square blocks are built around two airy courtyards lush with greenery. One of these blocks has an opening to the street, greeting the visitor with the restrained emotion of a columned hall. Behind that is an inviting sward of fresh green grass. Rows of slim concrete columns form the entryway while at the same time functioning as a visual link between the grid-patterned glass cubes. These cubes hold a very large volume, but their skin of glass and aluminium horizontals gives the massive office complex an optical lightness. From the outside, *Laccolith* appears like a delicate green, iridescent mountain range in the changing light of day. This, in the middle of an otherwise rather inhospitable architectural landscape. Visitors first walk through the columned hall. Glass doors open up to the right and left of a covered walkway. Behind each of them is a somewhat coolly styled reception area, from which the offices, conference rooms, a lounge, and a lecture hall can be accessed over the four levels of the building.

The overall grid pattern of 1.20 metre squares and a flexible room system are the optimal prerequisites for multi-purpose and economical use. This administration building does not employ eye-catching colours. Instead, it relies on elegant restraint. Grey and silver nuances dominate, while the materials – sandblasted glass, exposed concrete, and blonde wood – stay decently in the background. This reduction is the building's basic principle, proving once more that modesty is the clever daughter of architecture.

⌃ Various indentations enliven the façades

❬ Neutral materials dominate the interior

❬ The inside courtyard can also be used for breaks

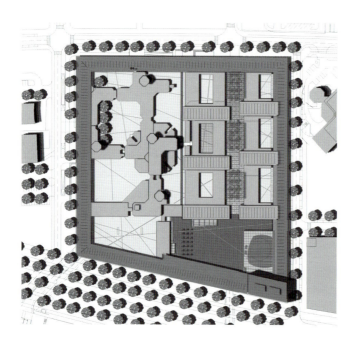

cultivation

work and trade

General Secretariat of the European Parliament, Extension and Alterations to the Konrad Adenauer Complex, Luxembourg

Architect
Heinle, Wischer und Partner Freie Architekten, 2014

The enlargement of the European Union in 2004 meant more space was needed for administration. The seat of the European Parliament's general secretariat not only had to be expanded; the work had to concentrate all its functions – which until then had been distributed over three locations in Luxembourg – in one central building. To this end, the Konrad Adenauer building was extended by 180,000 square metres and integrated into a clear, fundamental city planning concept. A six-storey perimeter block development provides the framework into which both the existing building and its annex are incorporated. And eighteen-level skyscraper on Avenue John F. Kennedy gives the General Secretariat's corner and functions as an anchor on the avenue for the development.

The extension adopts the 1.20 metre square grid pattern of the existing building, although the new building is given a different look by its different glass façades. The roof spanning the frame of the perimeter block development represents the unity of the European Union. The clear outer rim stands in contrast to the different types of buildings inside. Unity and diversity are the design's guiding concept. The public spaces are linked by a central representative square, the Place du Parlement, and a walkway between the existing building and the annex. The main entrance, the big hall, and the skyscraper are located on the Place du Parlement. In the double-storeyed pedestal zone along either side of the pedestrian area, a comb-like structure opens up. They rise over five levels with a glassed-in passage, putting rhythm into the linear space. The tops of these structures have been designed as communications zones and light up the passage at night. An "infrastructure level" serves as a linking platform for all parts of the building.

At the planning stage, special attention was paid to a sustainable building concept. The cooling systems, the intelligent use of natural resources, as well as the application of re-usable materials guarantee an exemplary net energy result.

∧ Various moods of light enliven the plaza during the evening

⌃ There is a front zone for informal meetings

vertical urbanism

work and trade

European Court of Justice, Luxembourg

Architect
DPA Dominique Perrault Architecture, Paczowski et Fritsch Architectes, 2008

The fourth extension of the European Court of Justice followed upon work to remove asbestos from the old building. An extension was intended to double the useable space: more than 10.000 square metres for the president, the judges, and the courtroom. In addition, twice that was planned for the translators in the two new skyscrapers that will make the court an unmistakable feature on the skyline of Luxembourg. A large auditorium, a gallery, bookstore and restaurants, a bank and a public esplanade are also part of the plan. Perrault's design took first prize in an international architecture competition as early as 1996. The first phase of construction dates from the 1970s and, with its almost Japanese-style metal façade, has a strong presence. The new building is located just below the old one. The Rue de Fort Niedergruenewald is to loose its character as a castle's defensive ditch. Because the court building has been enlarged every ten years, it not only reflects the architectural history of the EU, it also shows the growing importance of the court. The extensions now surround the old building. The Bailment Tower, which stood alone on top of the Kirchberg plateau for many years, was incorporated into an ensemble by the twin towers of Ricardo Bofill and made into a gateway to the Place de l'Europe. The second pair of twin towers, set at an angle to the others, frames a square together with the court building.

In order to unify the buildings as an ensemble, Perrault came up with a covered walkway linking them all. A peristyle acting as a filter on the ground floor makes the new building appear to hover. The interiors in the old building were completely overhauled; to make space for a foyer and the largest courtroom, the inner walls were demolished. The architect was not afraid to make grand gestures, at the same time taming them with clear contemporary geometry.

The façade is characterized by opaque and painted glass as well as by industrial materials. Symbolically and architecturally, the new building transforms the Kirchberg plateau into the Acropolis of the EU. The main entrance, once to the north facing the Boulevard Konrad Adenauer, was moved to the south. Here, a large courtyard near the Bâtiment Jean Monnet forms a counterweight to the Place de l'Europe.

› Glass and industrial materials determine the façades

⌄ The new parts of the building shimmer like gold

❯ The façade is characterized by opaque and painted glass as well as by industrial materials

calculated

Extension for the European Court of Auditors, Luxembourg

Architect
Atelier d'Architecture & de Design Jim Clemes, 2003

work and trade

This six-storey building for the European Court of Auditors contributes to the compression and urbanization of Kirchberg plateau and is also a substantial addition to the existing edifice. The almost one hundred metre long office block stretches along the Rue Erasme. On the ground floor are the entrance hall and a conference room for 150 people, a cafeteria, offices, as well as a connecting walkway to the existing building. A large conference hall extends into the main edifice. The core of the building, separated from the offices by two corridors, contains archives and space for electrical and plumbing systems. The upper floors contain interpreters' booths, discussion rooms and further offices. The two access ways lead from the main building to the entrance hall of the annex in the form of a glass corridor.

In the middle of the building are two elevators and a stairwell. The offices are reached via two parallel corridors. The flat concrete roofs with their cooling systems are held in place without girders. The large grid of slim supports guarantees a high degree of flexibility in the organization of the office space. The decision was made not to have suspended ceilings in the offices, making them pleasantly spacious, giving them more natural light, and an improved room climate. The façade with its projecting, light-coloured frame of prefabricated concrete pieces is divided into nine by three metre modules. The windows are room-high, and every office has a window that can be opened for ventilation. Horizontal blinds mounted on the outside can be moved to give shade.

The entrance is characterized by an eye-catching coloured pavement. The space between the circular driveway and the building is defined by a slice of wall, the extended edge of the façade. Meadows and orchards stretch out between the existing building and the new one. Near the conference hall, the different levels on which the two stand are bridged by a stepped garden. The conference hall itself has a rooftop garden.

↑ The bright foyer, flooded with light, is connected to the garden thanks to large window fronts

‹ The central conference hall presents itself in classic plenary distribution, equipped with modern event technology

exchange

work and trade

Conference Centre, Luxembourg

Architect
SchemelWirtz architectes, Luxembourg and Jourdan & Müller PAS, Frankfurt am Main, 2007

The conference centre, an ensemble of new and existing buildings, forms one of the three sides of the Place de l'Europe. It is made up of a large plateau incorporating a chain of enclosed units, some extending right across this horizontal section. The existing 24-floor tower building bestows on the complex a vertical dimension.

The plateau's units sit on a stone foundation and are enveloped in the glass hall with its overhanging roof supporting grass and vegetation. Extending outwards in a butterfly rim on the side facing the square, the smooth expanse of the roof swells slightly to mark the main hall below and also features islands of greenery that function as a counterpoint to the angular skylights. This "fifth façade" is fully visible from the higher surrounding buildings.

The 300-metre-long glass frontage facing the square provides a window on all goings on in the building, day and night. On the valley side of the building an additional membrane consisting of adjustable, frosted-glass louvres provides a shield from the sun and a measure of privacy during events where security is a prime consideration. This side of the building functions as a modifiable filter of the nearby green of the valley. The existing elements – Halls A to E and the tower building – are now unencumbered by adjacent structures and have their own distinct characters. The hall's enclosed units begin at the pointed end of the hall with the translucent Belvedere element that appears to float on a series of inclined supports beneath the spreading roof. Next comes the two-storey main hall in the form of a truncated ellipse. It is composed of tilting, wooden shells, the spaces between the shells accommodating auxiliary services. A panoramic window looks out over the valley. Where it butts against the main hall the existing tower building has been stripped back to its base structure. Additional openings in the tower's ceilings extending right down to the lower level of the street on the valley side of the building serve to accentuate the vertical component. Stone facework is being used to incorporate the two components of Halls A to E into the complex. The stone base, several storeys high and housing utility rooms, function rooms and parking facilities, forms the foundation of the building. Partially overhanging the Rue du Fort Thüngen, it rises above the lip of the slope, ending on the level of the square. The base recedes to become a plinth wall sheltering the approach to the underground car park and lining the peaceful interior patio of the dining halls.

‹ The roof projects far outward towards the square

˄ The glass façades allow views of the interior and towards the outside as well

˄ Inclined pillars create a lighter impression of space

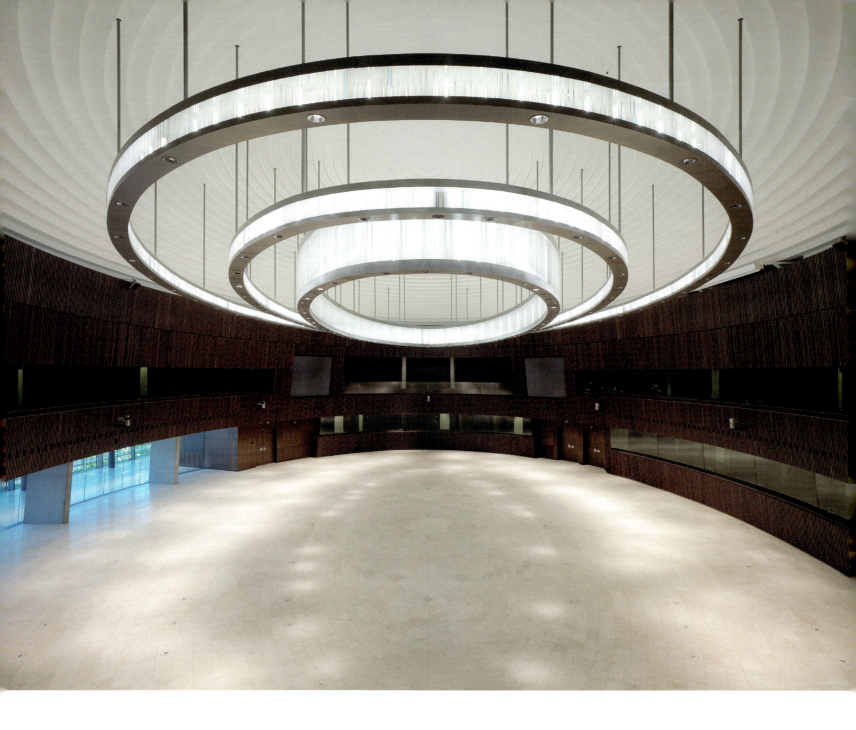

⌃ The lighting lends an air of ceremoniousness to the hall

❯ Large foyers are in front of all the halls

⌄ The office building emanates calmness at a hectic location not far from the motorway

independent

work and trade

Heights Offices, Luxembourg

Architect
P.arc Luxembourg s.à.r.l. – Partnership for Architecture, 2005

The H2O office block (Howald Heights Offices) is located in the Hesperange district on the southern fringe of the city of Luxembourg. Wedged in an angle between the motorway and Rue de Gasperich, the immediate environment of the building is one of transition and hectic bustle, the office complex itself appearing as a solid anchor and orientation point. The building, consisting of three 4-floor wings exudes a calm autonomy. It is a building block in waiting, timeless in design and thus generous in the leeway it grants the architects of tomorrow's surrounding structures.

The individual, interlocking units of the complex make up a sculptural ensemble. A large patio forms the central focus of each wing of the building. The bright interior space with its flowers and shrubs also provides the climax for this "verticalisation" of the office landscape. Shut off from the din of traffic outside, it serves as a focus for the surrounding workplaces. All floors are open-plan and can be easily extended. An axial "rue intérieure" provides access to the building from outside and the entrance halls to the various wings of the building lead off from it. Movement between floors is via three lift shafts and stairwells positioned at regular intervals. The dual-shell façade is the optical calling card of the building. The interior thermal layer provides floor-to-ceiling glazing with individual windows. Its shell, likewise floor-high, is of green-tinted glass panels. These are set at a slight angle into a concrete cantilever slab and block out the noise of the traffic.

Thermal ceilings and an anti-glare membrane between the two shells make for a pleasant work environment. From the perspective of a passing car the office complex's façade changes from closed to transparent. The immediate outside environment is reflected in this glass frontage of subtly changing colours. The powerful aura of the complex, the detail of its design, the physical quality of the structure and the architects' determination to create first-class and affordable office space in an autonomous building … all these factors have established the H2O as an important example of office block architecture. The developer of the complex was Luxembourg Office Solutions.

˄ There is a patio on each wing

↑ **The architects consider the building to be a "component in a state of waiting"**

solid

Rehab centre "Rehazenter", Luxembourg

Architect
m3 architectes
Dell, Linster, Lucas, 2007

work and trade

The design of the rehab centre reflects the building's function and location. It is composed of three sections, dedicated to therapy, the connecting structure and in-patient wards respectively. The various therapy rooms are located at garden level. All areas of the centre open to the public are on the ground floor. As the building is designed for handicapped access and the ground it stands on is longitudinal in shape the complex is extended in the horizontal plane.

The therapy rooms are lit and ventilated by means of strip windows and four interior patio areas, each with its own design. The sports hall and the large swimming pool are embedded in the patios like a room within a room. An auditorium, coaching rooms, a restaurant and the centre management offices all branch off the foyer. There is an unobstructed line of sight between the sports hall and swimming pool and these areas, which are in turn connected to the administration offices, the doctors' surgeries, the medical engineering department and the neurological rehabilitation/cognitive psychology department. The underlying structure acts as a supporting backbone for the rest of the building. The complex acquires a dynamism from the various longitudinal façades. The glass front on the north side facing the approach to the centre bestows a transparency on the glazed interior concourse. The south-facing side is in the form of a punctuated façade, many small apertures in the exposed concrete providing glimpses into the various therapy areas.

The three in-patient departments are geometric box-type structures that penetrate the supporting base of the building and are situated above the therapy floors. All rooms use warm building materials and colours with a view to making the patients' stays as pleasant as possible. Materials have been kept simple and were used in modest quantities. All public areas feature exposed concrete, screed floors and metal window frames and doors. In the rooms and wards the window frames and floors are of oak.

The area in front of the centre is partially frequented by the general public and links the premises to the surrounding residential and commercial district.

⌃ All public functions are on the ground floor

> Various interior courtyards create natural lighting and ventilation

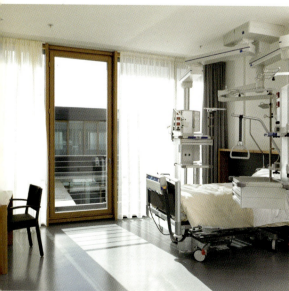

open space

SES, Botzdorf

Architect
Christian Bauer & Associés Architectes, 2000

work and trade

The design for the head offices of the satellite company SES was decided by an architecture competition. The winning design, however, exceeds the stipulations of the competition. The architects were keen to find a suitable symbol for this successful company and integrate the building harmoniously into the delicate natural environment. The straggling plot of land features a mansion situated next to a wood in the rolling countryside. A plateau with gently curving walls links the mansion to the new ring-shaped building.
A garden serving as buffer zone between wood and meadow conceals the car park, a potential site for a future building.
The plateau, partially embedded in the ground, opens up on the valley side and houses multipurpose rooms, the kitchen and the restaurant. The new, two-storey ring construction accommodates all departments and provides scope for a variety of spatial configurations.

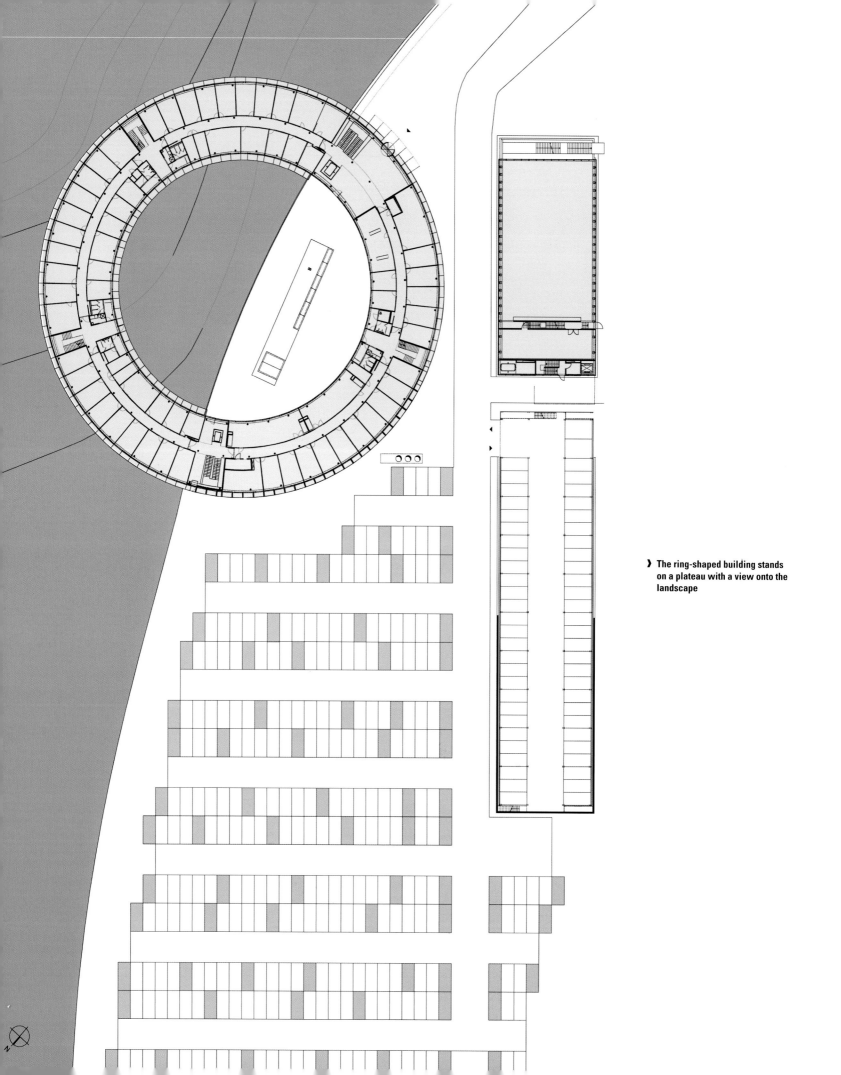

› The ring-shaped building stands on a plateau with a view onto the landscape

opposites

Soteg, Esch-sur-Alzette

Architect
Atelier d'Architecture &
de Design Jim Clemes,
2006

work and trade

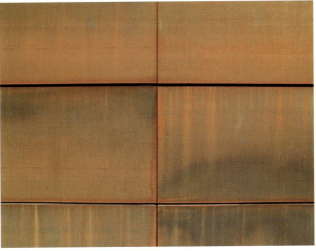

The Soteg project took as its design theme the relationship between history and the present, recollection and the future, tradition and innovation. The architects were keen to preserve this magical location at the heart of an industrial wasteland and set about creating "a landscape, a geography, an identity" out of the interior of this future Schlassgoart enterprise park.

A former gas-fired power station became an office complex while the old pumping station is now used as a conference room. These two entities stand in relation to the new workshop building and provide a commentary on the location and its history. More than this, however, they herald the shape of things to come, first and foremost the development and integration of the Schlassgoart enterprise park in the heart of the town.

⌃ The area is marked by the contrast between old and new

↖ The new construction breaks away from customary industrial architecture in its choice of façade materials

‹ Just a few modern ingredients are enough to breathe new life into the old gasworks

⌄ The details of the renovated buildings and new buildings are just as solid as those of the old buildings

extra bancaire

banks

Annex for a Bank, Luxembourg

Architect
Atelier d'Architecture &
de Design Jim Clemes,
2002

The purpose of this annex for a large bank was to restructure the interior, to create new offices and a space for exhibitions, and to give the reception area on the ground floor its own link to the street. The architecture in the new annex emphasizes the modern, and reveals neither continuity nor mediation in reference to the other buildings in the area. Its vocabulary and composition are not in contradiction with the neighbourhood, but they are an expression of technological complexity. A large part of the planning energy went into designing the façades, which are to not only be the new face of the bank but also a landmark in the city. Their execution is complex, but the result is clear and comprehensible. The levels of the building are held up by exposed girders. The ceilings hold the entire edifice's heating, ventilation, and air conditioning – all needed for the optimal circulation of air. The façade is detached from the supporting structure and can be seen at a number of points inside the building in its full dimensions as a supporting element. The contrast between the work rooms and the heavy pillars, ceilings, and walkways is underlined by the energy-efficient double façade, whose mobile blinds can make it transparent or give it a phased-in opacity. Thin slats of white, slightly speckled marble are set, protected, between the panes of glass. The pale marble breaks the sunlight, ensuring a pleasant atmosphere in the interior, which is never too light or too dark. The outer façade of plain glass is arranged like shingles and suspended from steel cables. The cables also support the façade's maintenance platforms. The inner façade is attached to the concrete shell of the building and is made of soundproof glass. The space between the inner and outer façades is sufficient to regulate ventilation and to protect the offices from getting too much sunshine. The dialogue between glass, steel, and marble gives the interiors a harmonious balance. Curving suspended walkways cut dramatically through the space on several levels, providing access to the corner offices. The façades underline the difference between the closed, discreet offices and the generously-sized transitional areas; they also provide a panoramic view across the city.

⌃ Frameless glass façade

> The roof terrace allows for a view onto the roofs of Luxembourg

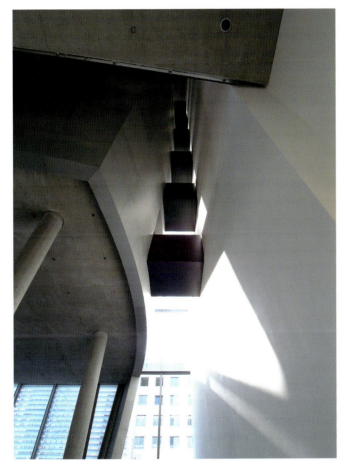

> View to the opposite side of the street from the walkways

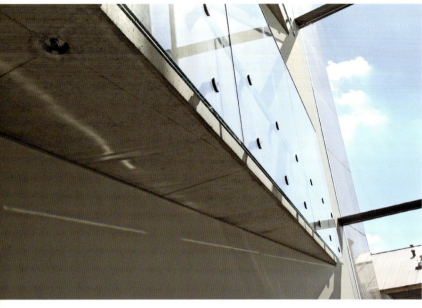

Glass, steel and marble provide a harmonious connection

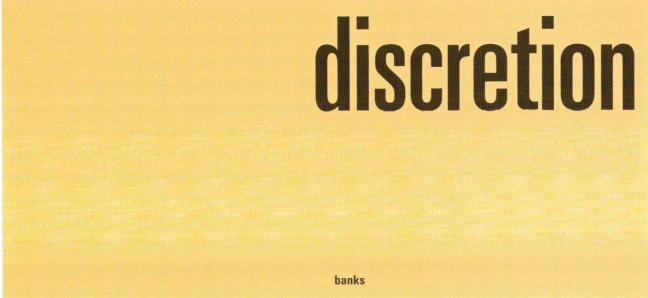

discretion

Commerzbank Luxembourg (CISAL), Luxembourg

Architect Hermann & Valentiny und Partner, 2003

banks

A first impression of the building is a matter of seconds: driving along the clearway, you glimpse, through a gap in the streetscape, the deep, dark entrance of a pale edifice with palm trees. While you are still asking yourself whether you are suffering from a trick of the senses, the car turns into Rue Edward Streichen. Only here does the sculptural white building really become visible. A broad roof spans its two sides, separated as they are by the deeply-carved entrance. The sharp-edged building, five storeys high and almost a hundred metres long, is different from its neighbours.

It follows the principle of perimeter block development, taking up the edges of the surrounding buildings while still managing to be different. The banking houses here often do without large, impressive entrances, because not a few of their clients demand discretion and prefer to enter via the underground car park.

But the architects of the Commerzbank wanted to give the building a face – a deep, funnel-like cut into the façade marks the entrance, which is open along the entire height of the building. To underline its importance, the architects had dark brown wooden panels mounted along parts of the façade and the underside of the roof. They form a sharp contrast with the abstract white prefabricated concrete elements and strengthen the attraction towards the entrance.

Sunlight enters via the partially glassed-in area: two ponds flank the visitor's path to the foyer. The sound of water bubbling and falling drowns out the noise of the street. With the windows open, the splashing of the small fountains can be heard even in the highest offices.

Galleries open onto the foyer, which lives from the interplay of strong colours. The walls are covered in dark wood panels; red-painted gaps between them put a fine web of horizontal lines over the walls and stress the fine grain of the wood. The natural stone floor of light-coloured Spanish marble forms a harmonious contrast. Given its expressive details, the atrium with the polygon skylight, through which you can see the sky and through which the sun penetrates into the tall space, could be a theater foyer. The reception desk, which is made of the same honey coloured marble as the floor, is minimalist and abstract; a sheet of frosted glass has been placed in front of the red-painted concrete wall behind it; the glass is lit from beneath, creating a shining, eye-catching feature.

Three long, drawn-out wooden figures by Walter Schembs, each turning its eyes to the ceiling, stress the height of the space. They stand near a tree that grows out of the stairwell from the underground car park into the foyer – the only adornment of this space.

Visitors, clients, and employees enter the building via separate entrances and move through it along different channels. Unexpected meetings can be avoided. Making that work without turning the building into a labyrinth was one of the challenges facing the architects. Separate elevators for customers and employees ensure that they will not meet. Projecting terraces covered in plants create a visual distance to the normal offices, so that the private customer is also protected from prying eyes.

The back of the building is laid out as open space which can be accessed via the canteen. The latter, with its large glass surfaces, opens onto a quiet garden with trees and bushes, in which employees can sit and relax during their lunch break. A long pond with water-plants in it reinforces the private atmosphere; a pergola of patterned white concrete pillars forms a border between this area and the street.

⌄ The vertical façade is illuminated during the evening, creating a special mood

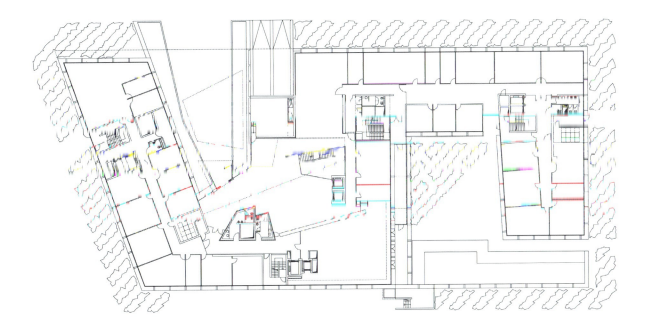

▲ Floor plan

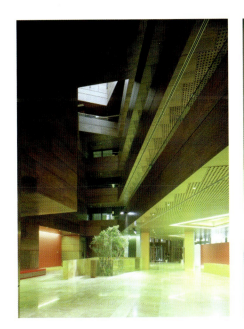

❬ Walkways open up to the inside courtyard

anthracite

banks

IKB International, Luxembourg

Architect
HKW Hhöää Köllörmänn Wawrowsky Architektur + Stadtebau, 2004

As the first of a row of four equally large buildings, the IKB – located directly on an intersection – has a special role to fill in the area's town planning. The outline of simple cubes set out in the development plan proved to be a clever strategy. The small but precise forms, with their strong presence in the cityscape, allowed the edifice to hold its own against the larger buildings on the opposite side of the street. The IKB's architectural concept reinforces the intention of the predetermined urban development plan by placing its faith in the natural strength of a massive cube. Giving expression to the bank's plan for the use of space and the characteristics of the area took priority in all the decisions regarding proportion, the choice of materials, colour schemes, and structure. Along the downward-sloping edge of the street, the level of the adjoining, shiny gold plastic runs horizontally. The meeting of the two levels causes the northwest half of the bank plateau to sink into the earth, while the southeast, exposed half rises above its surroundings as a wedge-shaped golden pedestal. At the intersection of the two levels is the entrance to the bank. The separation of the entry level from the outside world by a gap to the street – broader in the case of the public Rue Erasme and narrower towards Rue Léon Hengen – underlines the exclusivity of the institution. The design of the ground floor also formulates the public attitude of the bank. Above the pedestal is a simple block. The architects were sparing of their means of expression. The reduction to a stone, anthracite-coloured block allows the building to rest in itself. When the sun shields of matte shining shutters is employed, the mass of the block appears to contract – to a form of quiet energy.

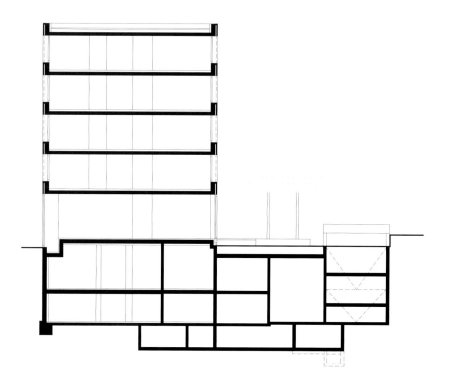

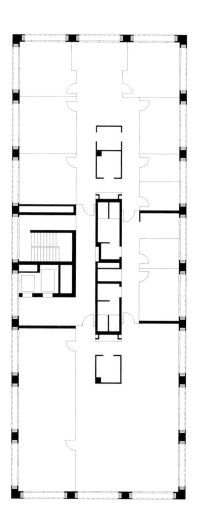

❮ Section and floor plan

❰ The abstract cube

❰ The rear square is illuminated during the evening

❰ The colour concept accentuates the inside areas

certified: very good

European Investment Bank II, Luxembourg

Architect
Christoph Ingenhoven,
2000

banks

The European Investment Bank (EIB), one of the most financially powerful banks in Europe, finances European Union projects. Its new building is to be constructed on Kirchberg plateau, next to the bank's main administrative building, designed by Sir Denys Lasdun in 1980. The land intended for the extension adjoins the existing property and gets its character from the city on one side and the countryside on the other. A V-shaped, curved glass shell spans the two office complexes, which are linked to one another by atriums and covered gardens. Underneath this shell, the design focus of the old building – namely the terracing – is interpreted anew, because it mediates between the two edifices without copying the old one. The design adapts to the topography of the land on all sides, fitting into the landscape well. The lie of the land is reflected in the interior of the building also – the halls and the restaurants, conference rooms and public areas are all located on "landscaped terraces." The office levels are characterized by their flexible structure. Communication and spontaneous interaction are promoted by open, jointly-used spaces at the interfaces of the departments, which can be freely combined. The covered gardens ensure natural ventilation of the offices and reduce energy use at the same time.

The glass halls outside the offices function as buffers against the weather and are an important part of the energy concept. The EIB will be the first building in continental Europe to receive the certification "very good" under the EAM environmental standard of the UK's Building Research Establishment. Within its area of about 70,000 square metres, the building integrates all the special functions of the main administration along with additional work space for some 800 employees.

▲ Three atriums each point towards
the street and the valley at the rear

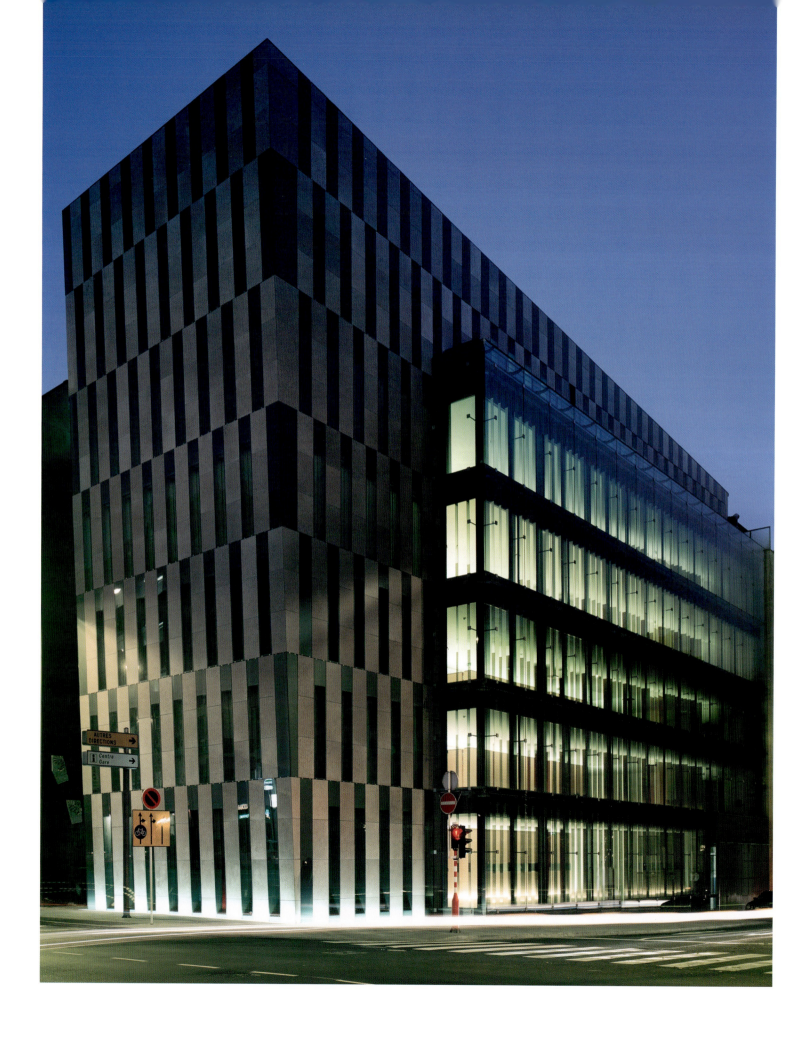

central

Zentralbank II, Luxembourg

Architect
Christian Bauer &
Associés Architectes, 2000

banks

The concept behind the Luxembourg Bank's Monterey Building was informed by the dual constraints of its integration into the urban environment and its character as a unique architectural entity standing out from the surrounding buildings and underscoring its own independence – and, by extension, that of the Central Bank. This duality demanded that the Monterey Building both fit in and stand out. The bulk of the building is comprised of two sections. The stone structure with its obliquely positioned apertures, emblematic in their effect, is a response to the Avenue Monterey with its traffic and the unprepossessing spectacle that it presents. The tapering design emphasises the building's corner location. The glass structure on the other hand is the architects' response to the park opposite the building. Its double façade with glass louvres provides sufficient protection from the glare of the sun without compromising on transparency. The ground plan is built around two supporting cores that take up the adjacent rooms and allow the office floors a measure of flexibility in their configurations. The ground floor houses a numismatology museum. The higher-ceilinged section on the top floor serves as a multi-purpose hall. The adjoining reception area can be transformed by a retractable mechanism into a number of lecture spaces complete with monitors. Stone and wood dominate; red surfaces abound. The stone, imported from Burgundy, was selected for its character as reflected in the claret-coloured veins of the material; it forms part of both the façades and the floor. The weight-bearing cores are concealed behind oak panelling, which provides a warm contrast to the red doors and columns of the museum. The design of the entrance – a series of inclusions stamped with 1-euro coins from the countries of the Euro zone – alludes to the function of the building. Fragments of former sandstone window frames, embedded in the black concrete of the end façade, are a throwback to the old building. The design envisaged reconciling materials with geometry by considering both micro details (coins) and macro aspects (volumetry).

⌃ One senses the height of the
building in the common room

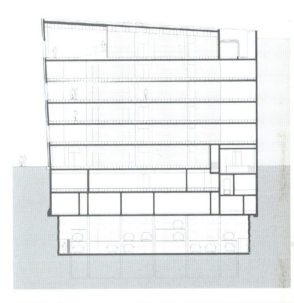

↑ The office levels are orientated towards the neighbouring city park

basis

Banque Populaire du
Luxembourg, Luxembourg

Architect
Tatiana Fabeck Architecte
with Thomas Letondor
Architecte, 2003

banks

Most designers of banks are preoccupied first and foremost with the issues of status and security. The architect of the Banque Populaire building, however, approached the challenge from the angle of urban design. A number of roads serving the city of Luxembourg converge at the roundabout on the Kirchberg. With its buildings dedicated to the service sector, trade and leisure the area is gradually becoming a district geared to the needs of the general public. Most of the surrounding structures are not "embedded" in the vicinity but rather resemble isolated "boxes". This strategic location for new developments at the entrance to the city is increasingly losing its character as a suburb of the city.

The stepped effect of the bank building gives the eye more to take in and gives the beholder free rein to imagine additions to the building in the future. The structure consists of two square-based prisms butting on to each other. The first building follows the frontage line parallel to the Boulevard Kennedy and has three upper floors. The second element has an additional floor and is set back from the boulevard. The building plant room, rising above the top floor, provides extra contrast and enhances the proportions of the structure, freeing up more of the surrounding area and allowing more light into, and better views out of, the upper-echelon offices. The fully glazed façades are the result of floor-to-ceiling glass frontages on each storey of the building. The same elegance and severity of style and the use of black and light grey colours also dominate the interior. The project, with its plasticity and fine lines, speaks the language of modern architecture. The frame of the building is not hidden from sight.

▲ Black and grey tones mark the interior

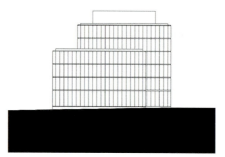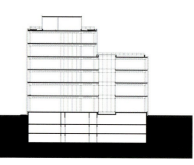

› Details and surfaces are austere and elegant

classy

Preschool and Primary School, Remerschen

Architect
Hermann & Valentiny und Partner, 2003

education

A school complex was designed for children from the districts of Schengen, Remerschen and Wintrange at the place where one drives into Remerschen. The ensemble of kindergarten and preschool with rooms for four groups, and a primary school with twelve classrooms is located at the foot of a sloping vineyard.

Wood, concrete, and glass were used as the raw materials, with a great deal of sensitivity. The rough edges of the poured concrete do not demand adornment in the form of graffiti; the wooden panels do not need carving, nor the glass surfaces scratching. The forecourts and the covered play areas are covered with untreated wooden planks. By contrast with traditional use, the glass surfaces in the walls cannot be opened for ventilation; but the wooden elements can. Sliding doors and built-in cupboards make it possible to change the floor plan of the rooms. The roof only vaguely corresponds to the school's ground plan and flares out on all sides. The classrooms are arranged at right angles in groups of two, with a shared special activities room between them. The walls of the music room, library, staffroom, administration, and toilets run at unusual angles, creating undefined spaces between the classrooms that are not solely for getting from A to B. They open up and narrow down to comfortable dimensions, creating an atmosphere that is beneficial particularly to relaxation during the breaks. The rooms for kindergarten and preschool groups have a bunk-bed feel to them. The materials in these areas correspond to those used in the school. Despite the differences, the ensemble retains its coherent, vital aesthetics – something every school needs.

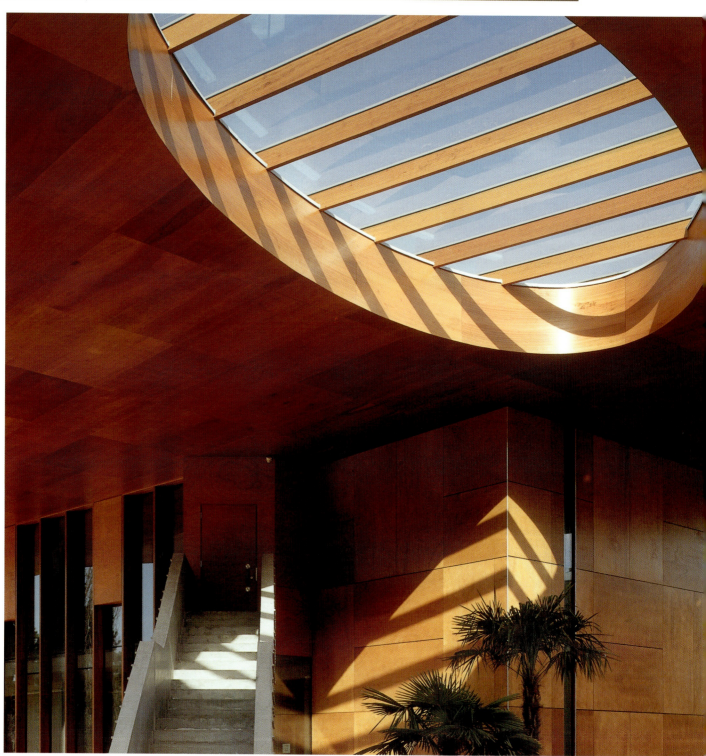

◄ Playful geometry marks the building

◡ Warm and cool colours and materials come together

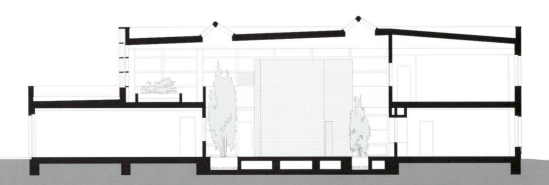

framehouse

education

New construction of a foyer scolaire and école précoce-préscolaire Hamm

Architect
Witry & Witry architecture urbanisme, 2007

An école primaire and a sports hall already stood on the parcel of land on the Rue de Hamm in Hamm, a suburb of Luxembourg City. The school building with its sealed-off schoolyard stands with its eaves parallel to the road. The sports hall was added later, parallel to the side perimeter of the land, without reference to the existing building, as was the parking lot at the end of an existing access road. The new foyer and school on the north-west part of the land form an angle and take their orientation from the old schoolhouse. The building forms a perimeter, creating a campus-like arrangement and giving the location an identity. The sides of the buildings frame a schoolyard on the south-east side. The single-storeyed foyer scolaire and the two-storeyed school are cubes standing at right angles to one another and are joined by an open, double-storeyed, glass-walled, wooden-framed hall. This part of the building with no internal supports has a span of twelve metres connects the foyer scolaire and the school and also serves as an indoor play area. The hall for the école précoce and the two halls for the école préscolaire are reached via this indoor play area. The two parts of the building – the massive construction and the hall – reflect one another in their dimensions and façades, and provide various spaces for the children to play in. The halls lead towards the indoor play area; they have largely glass walls and are equipped with sunshades on the outside. The multi-purpose halls on the upper floor are reached via a stairwell next to the entrance hall.

The foyer is reached via the entrance hall. The rooms for the pupils are reached via an access zone, from which one can go directly into the schoolyard. The rooms of the foyer are flexible in the way they can be divided up, and also have quiet work areas. The flat roof of the single-storeyed part of the building is home to a variety of plants. The hall's glass façade reaches up to the eaves, giving it a narrow overhang. All the secondary rooms have additional small windows – their function can be seen in the façade.

❯ Dense vegetation sweetens the short breaks

˅ Site plan

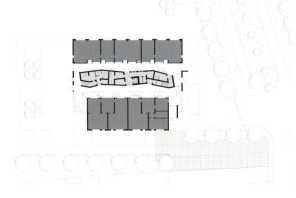

learn well

Preschool and Primary School, Eich-Mühlenbach

Architect
Arlette Schneiders Architectes, 2003

education

They have a saying in Sweden that "a child has three teachers: the other children, the teacher, and the classroom." Children spend a lot of their time in the schoolroom – years in which they not only learn facts but in which their aesthetic tastes are formed. The pre- and primary school Eich-Mühlenbach is one of those rare examples of how the gap between aesthetics and bureaucratic cost-benefit accounting can be bridged. The school is like a miniature town, with plazas, streets, and houses in which to live and learn.

The classroom here is no hermetic space; it has air and light. One's gaze can drift outside unhindered, but bands of glass bricks ensure it retains its contact with the inner life of the building. Despite the transparency, this is a quiet and protected atmosphere for learning. When you approach the school on the busy Rue de Mühlenbach, you will first see a long bar of a building of grey volcanic rock. Its entire area of 5,400 square metres is arranged in a staggered formation of two-storeyed cubes in a U-shape up the slope. There is a massive stone wall to stop the traffic noise; from behind it, deep red walls can be seen. A stroll through the complex reveals this to be a three-storeyed wing set at an angle to the others. It contains the entrance to the primary school, the common rooms, and an apartment for the caretaker. The preschool has its own entrance, which is marked out with tiny, coloured "peepholes." Open the iron gate behind the grey wall, and you will find the staircase ascending to the second level of the schoolyard. A clearly-structures organizational concept presents itself: the central yard is where the school's heart beats. This is where the view to the west opens up over the tops of the old trees in the park. From this point, you can see the preschool's main building, whose glass front opens it up towards the park; your gaze touches the sports hall and the primary school wing, oriented towards the green hill. A covered play area in front of it provides space for games even when it's raining. From this level, it is easy to keep an overview of the comings and goings. That is not just important for teachers on playground duty, it is also vital for the children's own orientation; because for preschoolers in particular to feel secure, they need clear paths, clearly-defined boundaries, and markers they can recognize and on which they can orient themselves. The colourful windows, which are shaped like decorative crenels on the inside, and the repeated motif of the pinewood underside of the covered areas, are such fixed points. Outside each classroom there are wooden fixtures providing enough space for jackets and sports bags. The wooden shoe rack also serves as a bench to sit on while changing your shoes. The coat and shoe racks are made of finely-grained blond wood; together with the shiny polished stone floor and the cool elegance of the glass brick insets, they define the classroom interiors. The windows in the primary school rooms face north towards the grassy slope. This architectural device allows plenty of light to enter, but leaves the rooms shielded from noise and excessive sunlight. The children have made little gardens on the green strip along the windows.

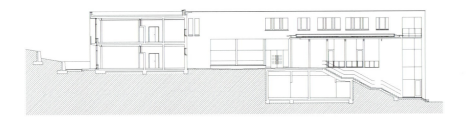

⌃ The corridor walls serve as a cloakroom

⌃ Four pillars mark the access

❯ Sports hall: daylight comes in above the collision screen

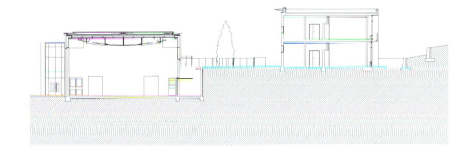

> The design shows the plunge of the grounds

eco-friendly

School in Born, Mompach

Architect
Witry & Witry
architecture urbanisme,
2004

education

The new central school for primary education is a three-storey building with eight classrooms. Thanks to its wooden construction, its accordance with lowest-energy standards, and the installation of photovoltaic cells on the roof, the school can justifiably garner praise as an ecological pilot project. A covered garden serves to conserve heat and forms a buffer against the weather. Energy-saving installations to regulate the building's technical systems help to significantly reduce energy use.

The building's orientation to the south enables an optimal active and passive use of solar energy. Walls, the roof, and the floors are very well insulated; the triple-glazed windows have specially-designed frames. The clever use of natural light reduces the need for artificial lighting within the building. And the use of hot water is also minimal.

The building has a heat-recovery ventilation system with ninety percent efficiency. Warmth is supplied via district heating, powered by a new woodchip-burning plant that serves all the community's buildings.

The covered garden is more than just an architectural windfall; it is a place for children to be when it's raining and where they can learn how to look after a garden. Plants themselves contribute to a better room climate. The glass façade lets in additional light for the classrooms facing north-west. In addition, sensors switch on the artificial light automatically as needed – this ensures optimal light levels in the classrooms. The barn-like building with its delicately-structured glass façade and the shed roof are architecturally linked with the nearby Centre Culturel, whose rooms are also open to the school pupils.

‹ A canopy protects the entrance

⌄ The roof is equipped with solar cells

⌃ Site plan

⌄ The school presents itself to the street with a large glass façade

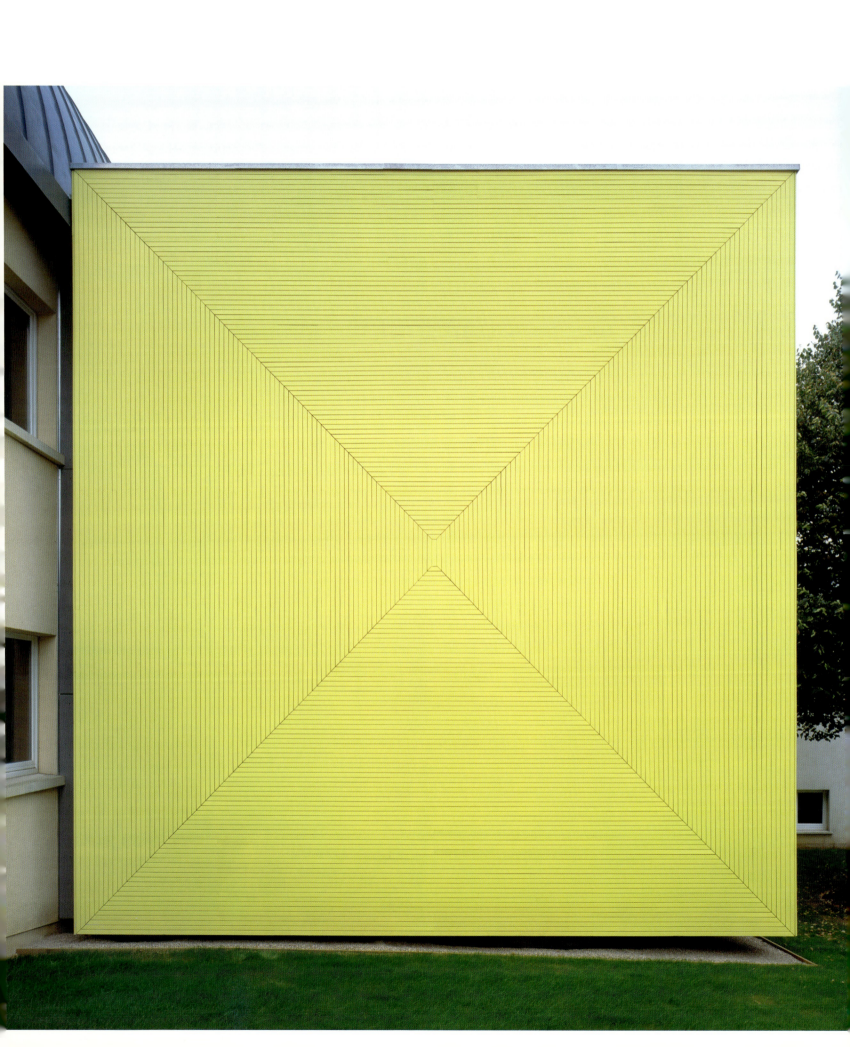

sportive

Extension of a Primary School, Howald

Architect
Bruck + Weckerle Architekten, 2007

education

Due to an acute lack of space, a quick decision was made to extend the school on Howald plateau by two classrooms, each seven by nine metres, and an additional group room. The new areas fitted into an existing, non-accessible courtyard and are reached via the corridors of the adjoining school wing.

A prefabricated wooden construction for the classrooms was put up on a reinforced concrete slab. The prefabrication allowed the walls, ceilings, and roof to be erected quickly. The new space was placed so that the roof of the existing school buildings did not have to be altered. The spaces created in between the parts of the building were used for built-in cupboards and technical systems for the electricity, water, and heating. The wooden façade is ventilated from behind and was given a protective coat of paint. The windows of the two larger classrooms face north – eliminating the need for sunshades.

⌃ The luminous colouring of the outer shell is continued in the interior as well

⌄ Band windows provide a view onto the neighbourhood

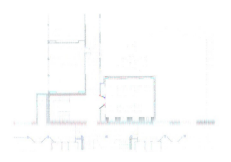
◠ Site plan

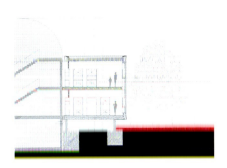
◠ Section

sunk in

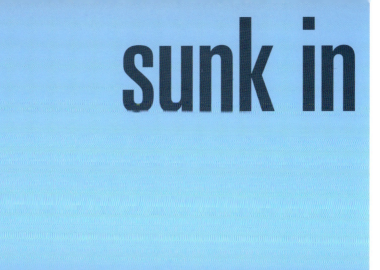

Sports Hall for the Ecole primaire Dellheicht, Esch-sur-Alzette

Architect
Witry & Witry architecture urbanisme, 2006

education

This sports hall with a covered area in front of it is located in central Esch and replaces another building on the site that was demolished. The covered area links the gymnasium with the existing school building parallel to Rue de l'Hôpital and forms the spatial conclusion of the schoolyard in the direction of the street.

The sports hall has a steel frame. The canopy runs over the covered area and keeps off the rain. Two wooden structures serve as access ways to the functional rooms in the sports hall's basement; they also form a secondary entrance to the school, incorporating an elevator. This area is heated. The wooden structures are clad in composite wooden panels; the windows have no frames. The covered area gets additional light via skylights distributed across the whole roof. A network of steel cables enwraps the entire steel construction of the covered area and the gymnasium. This standard multipurpose hall was set three metres into the earth and can be reached from the basement underneath the covered area, where there are additional sports rooms. The areas above ground are glassed in all round. Inside the hall, the steel frame covers two courts and the extension level was set inside, so that the weight-bearing construction can be seen from the outside. Plants grow on the roof.

The artist Sally Arnold designed the façades of the sports and break hall with a network of round, bottle-green pieces of glass, creating a lively, colourful play of light.

⌃ A view from the corridor into the more deeply-set hall

︿ Evening impression

‹ Section

harmony

Extension to the Rue du Verger Primary School, Luxembourg

Architect
Trisch-Olaster Architectes, 2007

education

The Rue du Verger primary school in Luxembourg-Bonnevoie required two additional school rooms and an emergency stairwell. The necessary extension also foresaw the addition in wood of a storey to the existing gymnasium, new toilets and showers, a multi-purpose room, and a separate entrance to the gymnasium from the street. The changing rooms in the existing gym were also enlarged.
It was planned that the extensions could be carried out without the need for additional land, while the schoolyard retained its existing form. In this way, the opportunity remained to further extend the building in the future. The new building, constructed to save energy, fits harmoniously into the existing face of the district, oriented as it is on the ridge and eaves heights of the neighbouring buildings. The new entrance to the gymnasium area was given a roofed forecourt, turning it into a bright, generously-proportioned foyer. Although the multi-purpose room on the first floor mainly serves as an additional staff- and storeroom, it can also be used for events organized by sports clubs, and as a visitors' box or cafeteria for bazaars and musical or theatre performances.

⌃ The wooden façades of the new construction harmonise with the stone fronts of the old construction

incorporation

Preschool and Primary School, Bettendorf

Architect
SchemelWirtz architectes, 2007

education

In 2001 Bettendorf Local Council invited proposals for the design of a school complex. The idea was to build a new primary school with preschool and kindergarten on the site of the old school in the village centre. The complex was designed with a view to integrating the new school into the village environment – as reflected in the height of the new building, which sits well with the old buildings in the vicinity. Standing on a newly terraced plateau, two angular buildings have been sited in such a way as to suggest exterior space in combination with the existing buildings. The surface of the façades consists of a pattern of plastered and fibre-cemented areas. The architectural experience is enhanced by the variety of relations created between interiors and schoolyard. Energy-saving buildings ensure that schools will retain their operating efficiency in the future. The school's multi-purpose hall also enriches the life of the village.

retaining value

Master Plan for Porte de Hollerich, Luxembourg

Architect
Teisen-Giesler Architectes
+ Nicklas Architectes
Luxembourg,
BS+, Frankfurt/Main,
Trafico, Vienna,
Stadtland, Vienna, 2004

urban development

In 2003, Luxembourg City held a competition to find the best plan for the development of the Hollerich district. From the 1970s onwards, the district had turned from being a vital working-class area into an uninviting corridor in and out of the city.
The 120-hectare space comprises parts of the Hollerich and Cessange districts and is largely made up of buildings with gloomy courtyards behind them. However, if made functional, the area could become a new gateway to Luxembourg City. Given the state of the city's finances, the aim here is to revitalize. A key stimulus here is the plan for a new peripheral railway station.

new middle

urban development

Redesign of the Centre of Hesperange

Architect
Bruck + Weckerle
Architekten, 2005

In early 2005, the authority in Hesperange invited five planning teams from abroad and at home to take part in a "consultation rémunérée" with the aim of solving traffic problems in the town centre. This key project provided an opportunity for a redesign of that centre. The already existing planning was to be evaluated and integrated. The challenge was for teams of city, traffic, and area planners to hammer out an interdisciplinary program. The proposals by Bruck + Weckerle Architekten, Vetsch Nipkow Landschaftsarchitekten, and Häckelmann Verkehrsplaner were recommended for continuation by the jury because they aim to "develop a new centre for the town using the special qualities of the landscape."

A double row of historical free-standing buildings currently ensures lines of sight in every direction and integrates the heart of the town with the Alzette meadow. The topography of Hesperange, specifically the broad meadow and the narrow mouth of the valley, were recognized as special qualities. The traffic plan foresees a redirecting and reduction of through traffic. The still-heavy traffic in the town centre is somewhat moderated using clever, low-cost redesigning of the streets and intersections.

The heart of the plan is a large new square as the town's focus, defined by buildings along the Route de Thionville. Festivals and other events will be able to take place here, within view of the road and the park. One building is to become the new cultural centre. The bridge over the Alzette – in need of redevelopment – is to be moved and widened. This will integrate the church square more firmly into the centre and raise its profile. The new bridge will also allow a redesigning of the overburdened intersection in front of the church. Construction of the first phase is to start in 2009.

Street and square area

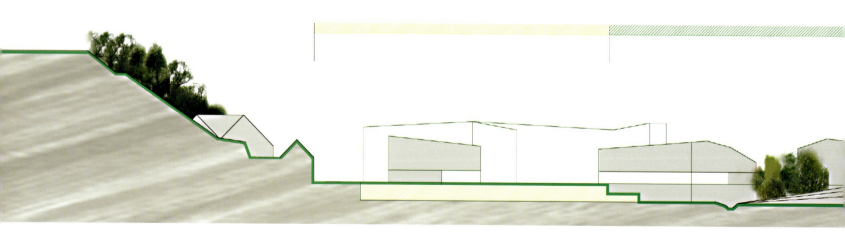

Holleschberg **Route de Thionville** **Public/private parking structure** **Cultural centre** **Itzig brook**

Landscape area

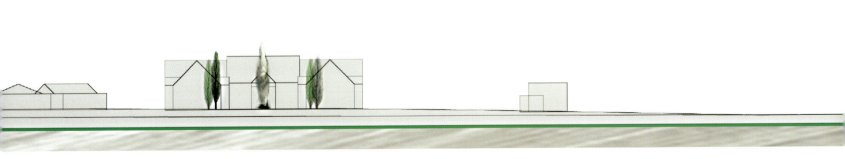

City Hall

new use

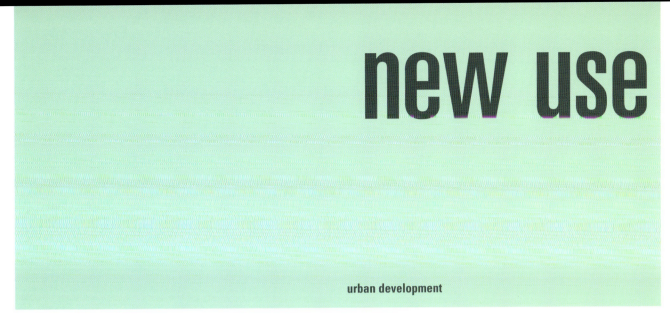

Ex-Industrial Site Esch-Bolval in Esch-sur-Alzette, Competition

Architect
Jo Coenen & Co.
Architekten, since 2001

urban development

This project shows the transformation of a more than 100-hectare industrial area into a town with 25,000 jobs and 8,000 apartments. The cornerstones of the urban plan are the two heritage-listed, 90-metre-high blast furnaces around which the different quarters and public spaces are grouped. The new steel yard relates to the furnaces; there are windows into the past and a central public square showing the original level of the industrial plant. The redevelopment required a new reference level for the area.

Blast Furnace Terrace: This area is dedicated to science, research, and university institutions. There is to be a concert hall here, the National Archives, and a centre for industrial culture. These investments will allow the furnace terrace to embody the metamorphosis from industrial to the knowledge society. The furnaces and the steel yard are rudiments that take on a central meaning in their new context.

Square Mile: Set out as a large square on what was once the steel production site, this is the district for services, shops, and town living. This is to become an address that radiates urban vitality and variety. Along the main pedestrian axis linking the steel yard with the park are rudiments of the steel industry: the sinter basins and the two chimneys form the historical backbone of the new quarter. The "Square Mile" is made up of a strict block structure in accordance with elements of the past. At the edges, there are like U-shaped tongs, creating a line of sight to the inviting surrounding landscape.

Park Belval: In compensation for the high density of the urban quarters, a green middle is created to guarantee the quality of life. This green space promotes the self-sufficient approach of the surrounding quarters, which all have different speeds of development. The park contains a few freestanding buildings; they are landmarks at the important points on the axes of sight. Set out as a "Fôret Sauvage," the park features the area's original vegetation and should be able to continue growing without additional care. As is often the case in developments of this kind, considerable expense is incurred in cleaning up contaminated earth. The Plateau St. Esprit, which already partially exists, is to be used as a central depot, artificially formed, and sealed. In this way, contaminated soil is used to create a topographic landscape feature that complements Park Belval in compensating for the density of the built-up areas.

Belval South: This residential area follows the cascade-like topography, reaching between the existing local centre of Belval and the park. The buildings in this artificial stepped landscape rise over a difference in height of around 35 metres to the park plateau. The formation guarantees wide views on the top levels and is the reason for a special design of rooftop terrace. Everyone living in the existing community can reach the park and the Square Mile via a central road and a landscape corridor, the cascades.

Belval North: The southern slope of the project area was mainly used for farming and was only extra space for the steelworks. Its meadow-like character has been retained within the new residential district. The typology of the U-shaped buildings makes it possible to look along long lines of sight into the park. This makes the proximity and accessibility of the green space the most important attraction. The patchwork landscape of meadows and orchards continues through the residential areas. The open courtyard of the buildings serves as a kind of stone island – a place to meet, play, and spend leisure time.

↑ The urban architectural model shows the desired density

⌄ The new constructions project
  from the old industrial plants

⌃ Something new is created next to the unused areas

interaction

urban development

Station District, Luxembourg

Architect
JSWD Architekten und Planer Cologne with Atelier d'architecture Chain & Morel et associés, Paris, since 2008

Architects submitting designs for the 2005 competition had the task of redesigning the district around Luxembourg's station and improving the urban landscape and traffic situation. The authorities were particularly intent on utilising the empty space next to the tracks, forging a stronger link between the isolated Bonnevoie district and the station quarter and city centre with a view to improving access from Bonnevoie to the main train station. As a main "port of entry" to the city the district around the station will provide space for investment and be transformed into a catalyst for the development of the broader area along the new boulevards and rail tracks. At the core of the project lies the roofing over of the railway tracks and the Bonnevoie bypass; this is the logical way to bridge the gap created by station and tracks. A park will be laid down on top of this "cap," the east-west axis forming the link connecting Bonneville with the station district across the tracks.

The concept was studied carefully over the course of 2007 and blueprints were drawn up. In the 27-hectare area under consideration planning permission is being granted for 366,000 square metres of gross floor area above ground. This area is destined for office, residential and commercial use on the fringe of the new Parc Gare Centrale, an expanse of greenery that will become central to the identity of the area as a whole.

The cap over the tracks is conceived as a composite steel construction, wide of span and virtually without structural supports. Designs for the cap and the park were studied and analysed by a team of engineers, architects, traffic planners and landscape artists. The eight-hectare Parc will be the new lung of the station district. Open spaces around the perimeter of the park, restaurants and cafes and the original rotundas will transform the rail facility into an attractive urban environment.

A network of ramps and flights of steps will provide multiple points of access to and from the park. Attractive sites for new building developments are planned for the fringes of the park, where provision is also being made for traders and retailers and a hotel, a cinema or bus station. A central feature of the cap will be the new, glass station concourse. A central, dispersal level above the tracks will improve platform access and new entrances will open up the neglected eastern side of the station to the adjacent district. The upper level will be flanked by 6,000 square metres of shops, cafes and restaurants. Large apertures in the cap will establish physical lines of communication between the green roof of the concourse and the hollow foundation of the park and will create a unique atmosphere for the train station. Travellers using the concourse as a hub for onward travel and wanting to access various points in the surrounding area will benefit from the new bus station, the underground car park and connections to an eventual tram service. The district will soon boast a main rail station that combines a modern transport facility with an attractive park.

The square in front of the railway station is intended to be freed, for the most part, of the above-ground through traffic

▲ A park is created above the underground tracks

▲ Daylight penetrates through skylights all the way down to the platforms

New construction sites are springing up around the railway station

loft story

Reconstruction of a Former Dairy, Bettembourg

Architect
Gambucci Architects, 2002

residential

Built in the 1930s and situated next to the railway line, the former dairy has been converted into a residential address. As is common with old industrial facilities, the rooms in this building are very generously dimensioned. This abundance takes on poetic value and proves not least how such architecture, which at first glance seems dull, can lend itself to new uses without its basic structures needing to be changed or reshaped. The project also proves that lofts are by no means an urban phenomenon and exclusively suited to young, liberal and, above all, childless households. The courtyard serves as a meeting and communication space for the residents; the open garden areas attached to the individual flats are not separated from one another by objectionable fences. The restaurant creates additional publicity. The entire project is the expression of a new attitude that is now gaining in popularity in Luxembourg as well. The architecture is enhanced through the clarity of the spatial capacities that were strictly preserved according to the design. The merging of flats in a complex whose form enunciates hierarchies and yet gives each part its own distinctive feature is the most difficult and, at the same time, most successful achievement. It has succeeded in enabling various functions such as a kindergarten, dental surgery, art gallery, restaurant, lofts, architect's office, real estate agent and so on to exist alongside one another. As the first example of the transformation of industrial buildings in Luxembourg, the reconstruction of the dairy serves as a reference model for other projects of this nature.

Impressions from yesterday and today

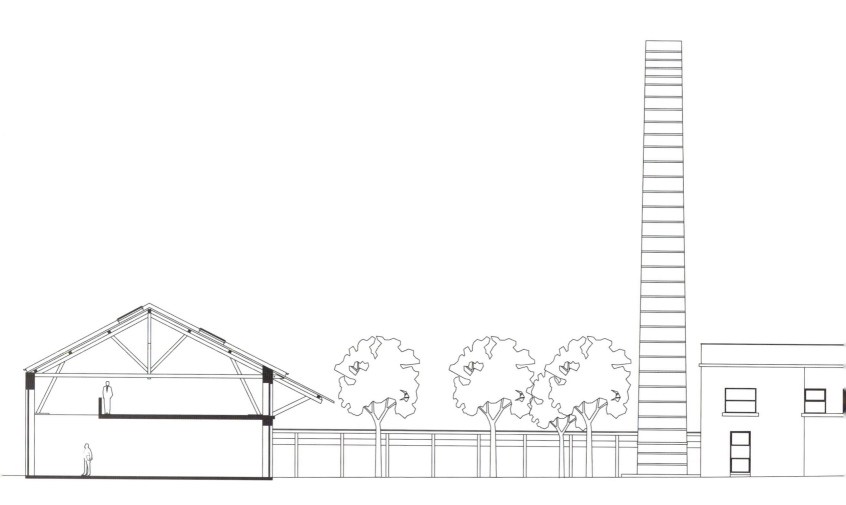

Living and working in the former dairy

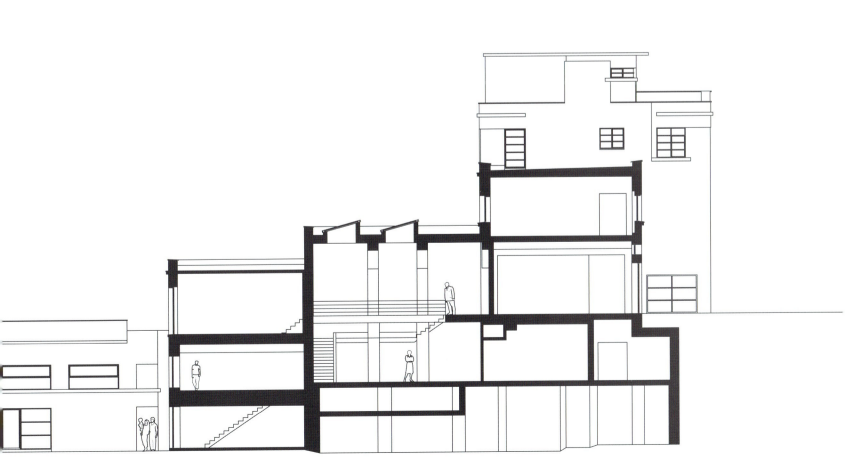

social

Social Housing, Bettembourg

Architect
Paul Bretz Architectes,
1997

residential

Located near the city park with its baroque palace, the district, for which Paul Bretz had a design plan drawn up on behalf of "Fonds du Logement", stretches out parallel to the railway line that runs through Bettembourg. A portion of the overall plan was carried out in 1995–1997 based on Bretz's concept.

The plastered walls in spotless white are accentuated by colour-harmonising window and terrace areas. The buildings pleasantly set themselves apart from their surroundings with their classic design vocabulary. The square top section is made up of three floors, each containing two-roomed apartments, which are accessible via an inner stairway. The flats in the building rows, on the other hand, are reached via a steel stair tower located at the front of the building that leads to an access balcony on the long side of the building. The adjacent lower rectangular structure contains maisonettes containing 1–3 rooms which have access to a terrace or a small private garden. As constitutive criteria the elongated buildings in the rear section feature a high, narrow bedroom window that looks like a vertical slit with two wings, while the living room allows direct access to the flat's own open spaces via wooden-framed French doors. This strict interplay already reveals from the outside where living rooms and bedrooms are located. The generous windows are orientated towards the western side; functional rooms such as the bathroom, kitchen and storage room, with their small windows, face the east. The architect allowed himself a special luxury within the cost dimensions of the social housing by raising the height of the ceiling in the bedroom area from the usual 2.5 metre to three metres. Although this alteration is hardly reflected in the total costs, as only two more rows of bricks had to be laid, the effect proved to be markedly appealing as the 10–12 square metres rooms were left with an unequally more spacious effect.

⌣ **Floor plan**

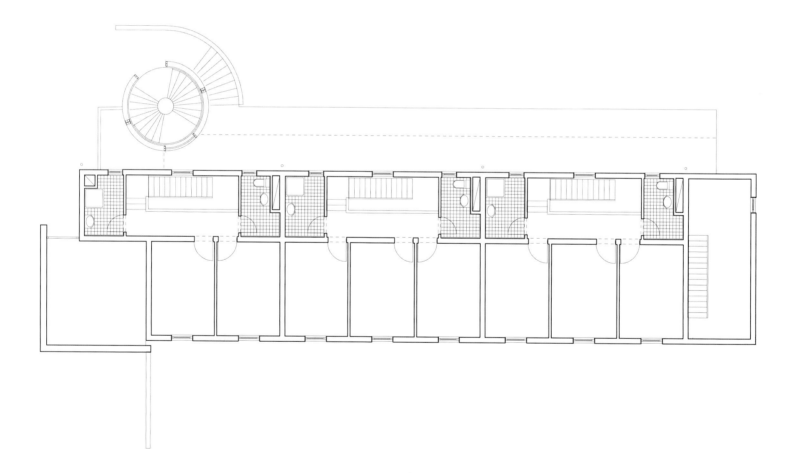

↳ The apartment buildings have an urban feeling despite the peripheral location. Wooden and plaster surfaces alternate with each other

monolithic cube

Maison Zambon, Dudelange

Architect
Paul Bretz Architectes, 2004

residential

The Zambon family's house would not have been able to be realised in many development areas where zoning ordinances specify mandatory materials and colour for roofs and façades. In Dudelange's development area the visions of the builder and architect of simple designs were nevertheless able to be implemented. The monolithic cube has a 30 centimetre thick shell of exposed concrete with form boards and appears closed. It rests upon a square floor plan with a grid of 4.3 metre that was divided again, having the effect of defining the size of the spaces in the living and bedrooms. A terrace was built on the front of the cube with exactly the same dimensions. The building is centred around and opens up on this terrace. From here views are offered of the roof scape of the town in the valley with its steeple and the silhouette of the Johannisberg.

In the basement there is a studio that is naturally illuminated via a small forecourt. The street façade has two recesses: The ground floor recess embraces the entrance and garage door while the second recess allows light from above to fall into the living room and offers protection from the sun and room for the chimneys through a set back glass façade. Through the recess an alcove spanning the width of the room emerges for a fireplace, television and cabinet in a built-in furniture piece. In the interior space walls and ceilings are plastered and painted white. The bedrooms on the upper level are laid with parquett flooring and the floor on the ground level with light-grey natural stone. The two-storey glass façade enables the interior space and the canopied terrace to flow into one another. The lower lying garden was clearly separated from the terrace by a surrounding retaining wall. Stairs connect the different levels of the studio courtyard, garden and terrace.

The rear wall of a pond and the circular bamboo hedge frame the garden and offer such a protected place to relax under an open sky.

Exposed concrete surfaces of an almost Asian austerity

⌄ Simplicity and clarity also dominate on the inside

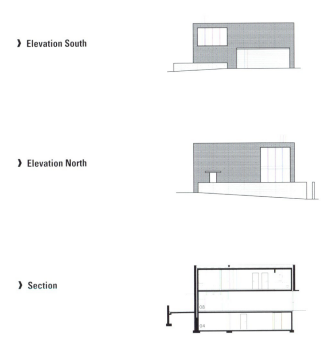

> Elevation South

> Elevation North

> Section

tree house

residential

Detached House, Bridel

Architect
Steinmetz De Meyer
architectes urbanistes,
2007

A house accessible from the street by a lightweight bridge was built on a sharply inclined piece of property situated in the woods. Thanks to this bridge, the rooms seem like a nest floating above the ground. In order to preserve the natural character of the grounds and its connection with the edge of the woods, the house consists of two parts: a massive volume clings to the given slope of the hillside like a grown tree trunk; the residing level hangs on this trunk like a nest, continuing as a projection in the form of a terrace.
The living area lies at ground level, searching for a connection to the tree crowns on the garden side. The residents can enjoy the location between sky and earth as if in a tree house. Large windows offer a view onto the forest. The walls of the flowing inside rooms appear free, not forming any closed angles. Daylight is led into depth through light-coloured floors and ceilings. The specially manufactured built-in furniture for the dressing rooms, kitchen and fireside room correspond to the architecture of the house.
The complex load-bearing structure allows for large windows on the ground floor. Two stairways, one placed above the other, divide the four storeys of the house: a concrete stairway connects basement and garage with the foyer; a second stairway out of more exquisite material, with wooden steps, creates the connection between the representative rooms at the garden level, including the guest room, office and library, as well as the private day-rooms and bedrooms situated above.

⌄ **A fragile trajectory mediates between the different levels, forming the access to the house**

⌄ The dining area opens up to the outside via a large glass front

operation esplanade

Conversion of the Site of the Former Tile Factory Cerabati, Mertert-Wasserbillig

Architect
Witry & Witry
architecture urbanisme,
since 1998

On the site of a former tile factory on the Moselle along the esplanade Wasserbillig, Witry & Witry designed a mixed infrastructure of apartments, offices and commercial entities that are orientated towards the model of historically grown cities with their mix of functions and density. A modern, car-free place with a high quality of living is to grow on an area of four hectares. The apartment buildings, consisting of detached houses, maisonettes, apartments, flats for singles and supervised social housing, adhere to clear cubist geometry. In addition to this there are shops, service areas and cafes on the ground floor and offices on the first floor. The planned pedestrian connection with the city centre as well as the public and communal facilities made available to the community residents are to contribute to the connection of the new quarter. A total of 120–150 flats for approximately 400 people are planned. The central residential street, nestled between detached houses and apartment buildings, is lined with shops, cafes, restaurants and offices and is exclusively for use by pedestrians.

The first stage of construction comprises four buildings of mixed use and 18 detached houses. It is marked by a discreetly accentuated and integrative colour and design concept. The flats on the third and fourth floors face the residential street with balconies and roof terraces. The solid buildings have perforated façades, flanked by two stair towers with zinc siding, while the ground floor features a façade made out of aluminium and glass. The four-storey office building has an austere perforated façade which is enlivened by the coloured aluminium blinds and the design of the stairwells. The service floor with its zinc siding and lightly slanted hipped roof represent a change from the roofs of the surrounding buildings. A five-storey residential building accommodates 18 flats with balconies or loggias that mostly face the Moselle. The white rendered façades achieve refreshing accents due to the coloured plexiglass balustrades of the balconies.

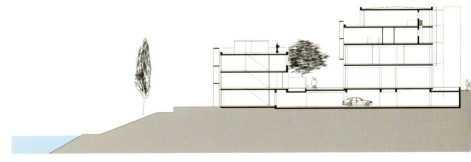

recesses

residential

Maison Schneider-Peter,
Peppange

Architect
Paul Bretz Architectes
2004

One normally associates building in the country with simple buildings, clear shapes and nature. An outstanding plot of land in both size and location situated on a hillside allows one to live in the open countryside and yet still in a village. Above, it lies close to nature and the surrounding fields; below, a view of the village with its convent and church opens up.

Initially, the house appears to be very introverted. The solid, almost closed external wall surrounds the three parts of the building with its U shape. The living space connects the guests' and residents' quarters. All three enclose the south-facing terrace that appears to be cut out of the building. These parts of the building open up to the terrace with windows that span the entire façade. The living space and terrace form the communicative centre of the house. This opening up carries over to the courtyard side. Two one-storey high recesses in the building mark the visitors' and private entrances.

The flat roof is, so to speak, the house's fifth façade. The demands on materials, detailing and construction correspond to those of a vertical façade. Also, a part of the planning task was the integration of the building owner's objects of art and to qualify the rooms as suitable backdrops for exhibits. The decision was made to use smooth exposed concrete that possesses the same quality as the external walls' material. It is concerned here with concrete members with a width of 2.4 metre. Two members form an upper floor. The members were manufactured on the construction site with a very high fitting precision and put together, the horizontal and vertical seams amounting to one centimetre. The ceilings, with their rough exposed concrete surface, form a clear contrast to the smooth external wall. The boarding works well for the acoustics of the rooms. All accessible and inhabited surfaces are laid with timber, both inside and out. The internal walls are plastered white. All recesses are extensively glazed.

⌃ A room for art

⌃ A view from the bath onto the open landscape

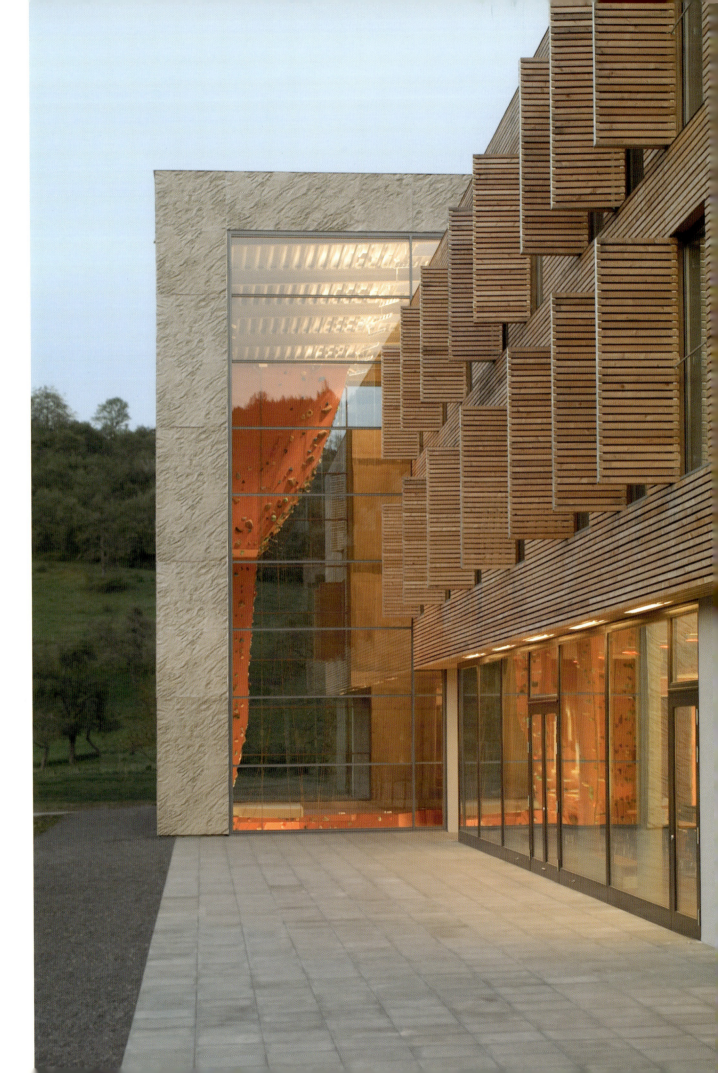

young and sporty

Youth Hostel, Echternach

Architect
Witry & Witry
architecture urbanisme,
2008

The new building for the youth hostel respects the continuous green wall that surrounds the Lake Echternach. Only a small piece of wood pushes through the border of trees and affords a view of the lake from the rooms.

The architects functionally used living and sport as a central theme in two superimposed building axes that continue into the open spaces. The sports facilities – sports hall, bike hire, climbing wall and tennis courts – run parallel to the street and wall and are marked by the climbing wall which is able to be used on both sides. The wing with dining and common area cuts through this axis at a right angle and heads towards the lake. The entrance and reception are located at the point of intersection.

A separate entrance enables use of the sporting facilities independently of the business of the youth hostel with its 120 beds. From the lake the cafeteria can be reached via a large terrace. The seminar rooms are also accessed via a separate entrance. There are open common areas past the entrance hall that open up a view to the high climbing wall. Apart from the kitchenette and lounge areas, these areas also provide access to internet terminals, a children's play area as well as a laundry and bathrooms. Placed at the top of the building were a seminar room and a meeting room that enjoy a panoramic view over the lake and are directly connected to the canteen via a second stairway. The living quarters for the owners are on the second floor.

A lower floor is designed for sports activities. The adjacent rooms under the entrance hall serve the sports hall, with its basketball court and grand-stand for 90 spectators, and the climbing wall. Skylights and side windows provide the sports hall with daylight.

The building was constructed to the ceiling and over the ground floor with a steel and concrete frame construction; the two-storey sleeping wing on top of it is a solid construction with wooden planking. While the façades of the sports facilities and the ground floor are shaped by exposed concrete and large windows, the exterior of the upper floors was clad with larch timber.

⌣ **Modern architecture which respects the landscape**

→ Site plan

→ Sports area and climbing wall

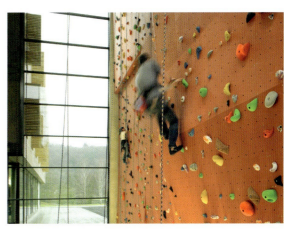

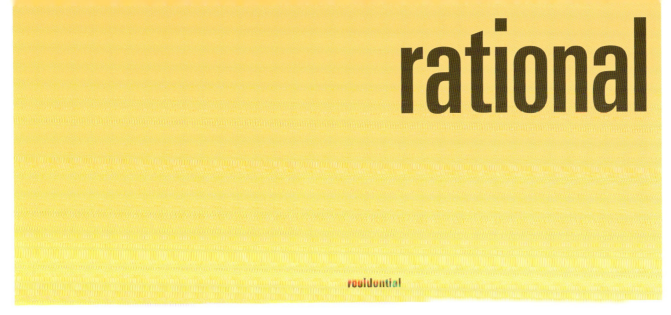

rational

Residential Estate, Bertrange

Architect
Dewey Muller
architectes et urbanistes,
since 2000

The architects built living quarters for normal life in its many different forms. In doing this they did not subscribe to the functionalism in the strictest sense of the 1920s but to a contemporary rationalism that takes into account changes that life entails.
The buildings grow in spacious stages aloft the southern slope. A harmonious picture emerges even though it is concerned with different living typologies with rows of terraced houses, apartment buildings and free-standing residential houses. The pastel colours – a soft, earthy red, ochre and broken white – are the first connecting element. The reduction of materials to plaster, steel and concrete also have a calming effect, as does the uniform colouring on the windows and doors.
Formally speaking, the concept of the Cité am Wenkel ties in with the housing development of the 1920s and 1930s. Examples such as the Neubühl housing development in Zurich or the Alvar Aaltos settlement in Kauttua were inspirations here. Typical is the layering of the structures on three levels: the uppermost level of the staggered living spaces closes with a flat pitched roof, giving the impression of a house within a house. Recurring motifs are the narrow ribbon glazing on the corners, the concrete beams of the canopies and the vertical structure of the windows. These vertical idiosyncracies reduce to a certain extent the dominance of the horizontal building masses.
Whoever strolls through the predominantly green Cité feels not least reminded of the concept of the garden city movement. Wide residential streets and narrow, loosely attached paths between the rows of buildings and terraced houses present wide visual axes and provide an optimal opening up of the view. Children immediately occupy this pathway system as a playground. Unlike most garden cities, the Cité am Wenkel is organically tied to the area. For all this, though, it remains a pure residential quarter without its own local supplies. Even though the area is more condensed than elsewhere in the country, the site in no way seems cramped. This is because of the privacy created by a sophisticated urbanistic space allocation plan. Laterally orientated garages form with the buildings small courtyards; dividing panels on the entrances and terraces of the terraced houses provide the "safe social distance". The concept of the outside area seems uncomplicated and completely natural but it follows a planned calculation that, above all, is based on the limitation of resources and the principle of repetition: stairs, edges and confined elements made out of coarse concrete and green hedges for the emphasis of the geometric contours. This alternation of wall and hedge, the layering of the space in rhythmic variation of openness and closeness, public and private space, shapes the entire quarter.
The architects see themselves in the tradition of Christopher Alexander who defined architecture as a product of elementary basic patterns which the morphological essence of a construction job is made up of. In the case of Cité am Wenkel that means: living is differentiation, it is orientation in the community towards time, and means recognising the house as an entity of life and constructed space.

⌄ The classic qualities of White Modernism: living in a green area and simple geometry

⌄ Floor plans

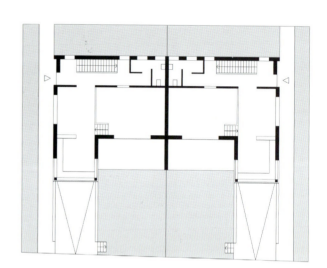

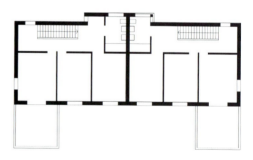

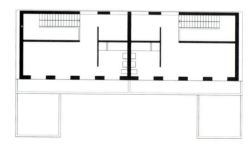

⌣ Gate situation ⌣ The loggias stand before the house like a shelf

quality of living

Residential Housing, Rumelange

Architect
m3 architectes
Dell, Linster, Lucas, 2006

residential

On the initiative of the city of Rumelange and the Fonds du Logement, a new urban quarter has been created at the site of the abandoned Rumelange–Ottingen railway line.

With the reclamation of an old industrial wasteland on the edge of the city of Rumelange, the project "Quartier de la Fonderie" does justice to the imperative of urban activation and consolidation, the most important societal and creative task of contemporary architecture and urban planning.

Row-houses, storey construction, office and business areas and several squares, together with the existing development on the Rue des Martyrs, round off the quarter. Row-houses, open carports, direct access to the garden and bright studios ensure living conditions suitable for families. The apartment house consisting of two clear bodies, with a slight bend in its ground-floor plan, is closely related to its environment – a wooded hillside and sheltered position behind the old railway-station building.

four seasons

Villa, Luxembourg

Architect
Steinmetz De Meyer
architectes urbanistes,
2007

residential

A detached house was built in a row-house neighbourhood of Luxembourg which develops very complex tectonics thanks to a large jut and a large recess. The white volumes are visually extended through strongly emphasised horizontal and vertical lines; the three façades "flow" formally together. The white of the façade strengthens the abstract character of the building, whereby the contrasting windows and panelling out of dark wood allow the outer surface to literally glow. The interior rooms form an organic, formally interlocking structure. The open living area on the ground floor extends over two levels and is connected with the office and the parents' rooms on the first storey. The interior corresponds with the garden, thanks to the large glass fronts, where a pool is also situated between the green areas. An outer courtyard interposed between the dining room and the living room creates a strongly interlaced quality between the interior and exterior: nature becomes a part of domestic privacy. This courtyard can act as an interior or exterior room according to the season. Thanks to its spacious window openings towards the south and the massively constructed weather sides on the east and north, the house fulfils the criteria of architecture which protects resources and the environment.

Open rooms and functional niches

vieille ville

Renovation of an Old Town Quarter, Luxembourg

Architect
Arlette Schneiders
Architectes, 2004

residential

The oldest part of the Old Town of Luxembourg has been restored and complemented with several new buildings. This quarter, with its very dense collection of buildings, is located directly behind the ducal palace and next to the museum for history and art.
Before the restructuring, the Fish Market was characterized by very old houses, small courtyards, and a huge block containing storage and exhibition space for the museum. Many of the buildings were used as carpentry or restoration workshops, and offices by the museum.
A new alley was to be created between the museum and the residential quarter. Arlette Schneiders' proposal won the 1997 urban planning competition held by the Fonds de Rénovation de la Vieille Ville. She drew her inspiration from the history of the place. The large courtyard was opened towards the Rue du Palais de Justice, in order to make it appear bigger. The street here is six metres lower. This opening also gives greater quality of life to the narrow east-west street, which is an extension of the main road. This alley used to only get sunlight for a short time in the late afternoon. The rebuilding has made it lighter because it now has an opening to the south. The surrounding district is also improved. Three courtyards were incorporated into the block. The houses in the Rue de la boucherie, and the house on the corner of the Rue du Palais de Justice/Rue de la monnaie, were restored and renovated. The buildings around the courtyard are new. The residential area may be reached via two entrances: one via an atrium on the Rue de la monnaie that links two old buildings and the new building. The second entrance is located on the other side in the new Passage *Gölle Klack*.

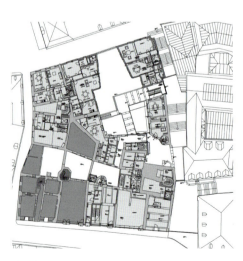

^ Site plan

^ The roof landscape is also orientated on the existing buildings

⌃ Section

⌃ View into the street

⌃ Old and new buildings form a harmonic ensemble

⌄ The urban façade of both villas is seen from the street side

at home

**Villa De Meyer-Fasbender,
Villa Freising,
Luxembourg**

Architect
Steinmetz De Meyer
architectes urbanistes
with Chris Fasbender
architecte, 2000
M. m. Architecture &
Associés, 2004

residential

The two villas, overlooking a sunny valley, follow local traditions of architecture on the sloping area in question. The De Meyer-Fasbender house was built on the foundations of a building dating back to the 19th century. The street possesses no pavement and has an irregular gradient. The entrance appears as a depression in the façade and is screened by a wooden wall.

The ground floor houses a garage, a playroom, a workshop and other utility rooms. The trapezium-shaped plot of land looks out in two different directions, with a flight of steps separating the two sections. Three bedrooms and two bathrooms make up the first floor. The main room extends inwards as far as the cliff. The façades at the rear are made completely of glass and give onto a small east-facing yard. On the top floor is the open-plan, glass-walled living room with a bridge connecting it to the garden. The kitchen, set back from the road, is situated between two large terraces with wooden decking. Prime considerations in the design of the house were the preservation of the original structure and its incorporation into a reincarnated building. The outlying areas give a surprisingly spacious impression. The same can be said of the neighbouring Freising house, which forms a single entity with the De Meyer-Fasbender house when viewed from the street, although it is more radical in its architecture.

The light structure of the building made it possible to open up the rooms and façades. The steps ascend at an angle contrary to that of the slope and parallel to the building's front. The rear façade is also glazed, with white as the predominant colour. Storage rooms are located behind the carport, which cuts deep into the façade. The cliff remains visible. As in the house next door the spacious living and dining rooms and the kitchen are situated on the top floor and enjoy copious amounts of natural light and also access to the terrace. This last floor is completely open-plan and boasts some striking furnishings. Close attention was paid to details, both indoors and out. The façades feature large yet slim-line window frames. The masonry of the walls marks the slope of the ground, the join with the building's base on the ground floor and, on the second level, the ceiling beneath the living room terrace. On this level the building is set back along its entire length to take account of the space occupied by the street. The large cantilever roof tops off the building in the style of the cornices of old houses. The ground floors and first floors provide the anchor for the two houses while the second levels serve as glass prisms, embracing the beauty of the surrounding landscape and providing views to the exterior. The dark tones of the plaster façades are in lively contrast to the bright interiors.

Rooms and façades open up towards the valley side

The rocks have been visibly left in the courtyard

wooden house

residential

Moko House, Schuttrange

Architect
Christian Bauer & Associés Architectes, 2007

This ideal location was once the site of a dilapidated wooden house. The plot of land is an extraordinary spot for a house – surrounded by trees in an elevated position on the side of a valley, with a range of views onto the fringe of the wood. The architects were keen to "preserve, integrate and recycle."
A new edifice has now sprung up on the foundations of the old building, whose original beams and wood have been re-used. Features include a basement designed to accept a garage and extension, a protective wooden annexe for the bedrooms and a glass pavilion accommodating a kitchen and living rooms and other living quarters. The interior décor is simple, with wood as the dominant material – ceilings, walls, panelling and parquet floors.
The large glass façades welcome the natural world into the interior living space of the house, which includes some tasteful elements such as pebble floors in the bathrooms and Corian worktops in the kitchen.

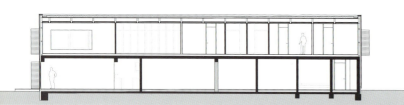
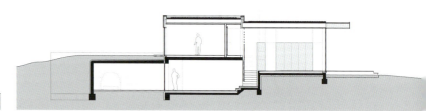

❮ The villa is partially situated on the foundation walls of an old wooden house

⌃ The interior rooms make a seamless transition to the woods

a living experience

residential

Avalon, Luxembourg-Kirchberg

Architect
Architecture & Environnement
Witry & Witry,
SchemelWirtz architectes,
Hermann & Valentiny und Partner
M3 architectes
Flammang, Linster, 2006

The Avalon district is the first new housing development on the Kirchberg since the 1970s. The plans are to transform the Grünewald and Kiemviertel districts and a Kirchberg dominated by office blocks and institutions into a lively, urban quarter. The new district takes its name from the ancient Roman road connecting Trier with Luxembourg and Metz, a thoroughfare designed by Munich landscape artist Peter Latz which passes through the Reimerweg park and features sculptures by Ulrich Rückriem. In its initial phase the project will see the construction of 380 apartments, with a further 500 following at a later stage.

The housing units were designed by five groups of architects, selected from among the entrants in a competition organised by Christian Bauer and Isabelle van Driesche under the auspices of the local urban planning authority. The architects agreed on a common material for the façades – red and black brick – which, in combination with a variety of other building materials such as plaster, wood and aluminium, will guarantee a consistent, unitary aesthetic for the development. The diversity of building forms, which include "L"-shaped structures and individual houses, has made it possible to create a district that, despite the high concentration of buildings, has an enviable amount of vegetation and many views over the park. The residential quarter is well served by public transport. Schools, sports amenities, a large shopping centre and the nearby financial district have all contributed to the success of the area.

- The houses were designed by five groups of architects
- 380 flats were built during the first building phase

clean cut

gardens and parks

Garden of the Banque de Luxembourg, Luxembourg

Landscape Architect
Wirtz International, 1996

Luxembourg is a city of banks: that is to say, it is a city of institutions who usually prefer anonymous buildings. The Banque de Luxembourg on the Boulevard Royal, however, stands out with its uncompromising, clear modern architecture of coffee-coloured stone, windows of toned glass and the wonderful Henry Moore bronze sculpture in front of the building.

The garden, which was laid out by Jacques Wirtz, is largely hidden and restricted to some 480 square metres behind the building: it is used for the recreation of the bank employees and their visitors. The front of the building is embellished with characteristic planting: three winding, trimmed boxwood hedges have been planted between the pavement and the building. They start off running parallel to the street but then move away, following a snake-like path towards the building. The main garden lies on the West side, where a semi-circular paved area is furnished with curved steps, gently leading upwards, to a labyrinth-like arrangement of 1.5 metre high yew hedges. On the North side, under honey locust trees spreading out between crowns of yews, a way leads to the hidden entrance of an underground garage.

On the other side of the garden, the bank has a second building – a superbly restored 19th century villa, which the garden links with the modern new construction. The steps up to the entrance of the villa are flanked by giant box tree cupolas, the largest of them being over two metres tall.

There are no flowers in the garden, only trees and hedges. They show how a limited selection of plants can be used to form a complexly structured, green space. Last but not least, the garden shows the ability plants have when it comes to breathing life into an urban space.

Nature is tamed by the gardener as it was during the Baroque period

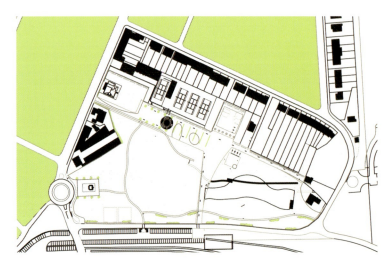

oasis

gardens and parks

Parc Jacquinot, Bettembourg

Architect
Diane Heirend, 1999

As the complaints about potholes increased in 1996, the Bettembourg local council asked the architect if she could do something about the roads in the Jacquinot Park and, at the same time, develop a proposal for the kiosk, which was threatening to fall into disrepair. As the idea of erecting a women's refuge in the park was raised, it was not a bit step to developing an overall concept for the neglected park at long last. The park had been laid out on a site four hectares in size, which had previously belonged to the chateau Bettembourg. From these historical buildings, only one has survived. A war memorial, a music pavilion and a small lake are the main features in the park: a camping site to the south, tennis courts and gardens to the East and a public road and railway tracks to the West form the borders of the site. The architect developed a sensitive and aesthetically coherent concept for the site, which concentrated on sensual experience and wellbeing. A bright yellow surface, permeable to rain, covers the consolidated paths and surfaces; two large grassy areas provide greenery and soft areas to relax and play and are made from a network of cast blocks whose colours correspond with those of the paths. The lordly trees define the volume of the park. The specially designed seats, streetlamps and waste bins (© atelier H2S) contribute to a unified appearance: moreover, the perception of the major axes is reinforced by the rhythm of the streetlamps. The two longer sides of the design were treated differently: to the East, a long pergola, overgrown with vines and climbing plants separates the public space of the park from the neighbouring private gardens, whilst West side is open to the road. There are three open spaces in the redesigned park: one is around the war memorial and integrates into the site; a second space is around the music pavilion, which is flanked by ten Norway maple trees and streetlamps, with a third, rhythmically interspersed by yew hedges, directly behind. It is clear that boules and pétanque can be played here – and this is not by accident. Two children's play areas round off the utilisation concept.

Despite its small area, this multifaceted site appears generously proportioned and radiates a quiet, unspectacular clarity. On closer inspection, there are wonderful details to be discovered. The streetlamps appear to have no light bulbs; light sources set in the ground highlight in the park after darkness has fallen.

The heart of the park is the small lake. The path along its bank meanders from a grassed area to a pile bridge over the sloping bank and reveals a pleasantly surprising view of the park greenery. The interplay between a viewing platform and the black concrete retaining wall between bridge and dam lead to an impression of distance.

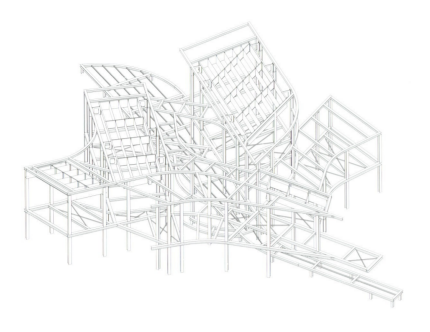

⌐ The play with colours strengthens the playful geometry of the Arcelor pavilion

colourful patios

Arcelor Pavilion, Esch-sur-Alzette

Architect
Miralles/Tagliabue – EMBT, 2006

pavilions

Several pavilions were built along the promenade running along the southern edge of the Parc du Centenaire to celebrate the one-hundredth anniversary of the City of Esch in 2006.
The Arcelor pavilion by the Catalan architectural bureau EMBT has been used as a gallery for art exhibitions up to the present day.
The starting point of the design is a piece of property located between a parkway and a "wild" natural park. The raised pavilion is located on an important urban axis and fits formally into the course of an extended parkway. A public area is being created underneath the building. The architects have developed the exact geometry with the help of pictures of minerals, chimneys, factories and a small church. The elevated path creates several colourful patios.
Additional cultural pavilions were conceived by architectural bureaus including Metaform (Economie, p. 294) and Polaris (Skip, p. 296).

transition

pavilions

Economie Pavilion, Esch-sur-Alzette

Architect
Metaform, atelier d'architecture, 2006

The Economie pavilion is one of three temporary pavilions which can be disassembled and rebuilt at a different location.
The basic idea of this design was to place a "floating" object in the park. Irregularly placed stanchions, taking up the motif of the surrounding birch tree-trunks, support a steel construction screwed together on location. A translucent membrane covers the structure, which opens up access via a ramp to the multifunctional interior. This membrane lets the daylight in, creating a direct relationship to the park through the shadows of the tress falling upon it. Illuminated from the inside, the pavilion has the effect of a great crystal at evening, thus functioning as a shimmering signal in the park. The interior, closed in front and in the rear by a glass façade, consists exclusively of rough, natural wood. Benches along the membrane offer sufficient accumulation space.
The low budget and the very brief planning and construction time (nine months altogether) were the essential deciding factors in determining the architecture. The membrane is an economical and quick solution to protect the construction from weathering during the building phase. The rounded-off corners of the steel bars make it possible to tighten the membrane without damaging it on the one hand, and, on the other hand, to lend the necessary lightness to the appearance of the pavilion. The materials have been used in their original form, so that they can be used again after the later dismantling without any problems.

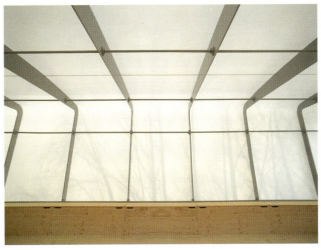

⌣ The interior rooms of the pavilion
  can be subdivided if so required

silhouette

Skip Pavilion, Esch-sur-Alzette

Architect
Polaris Architects, 2005

pavilions

This pavilion was designed and built as an information point, exhibition hall and lecture hall for the large planning area in Belval during the course of an open competition. An open area of about 400 square metres extends out in the Skip pavilion; it can be divided, separated or left open as needed. The shape of the pavilion is used as a logo by the owner – its special quality attracts the public without revealing the secret on the inside right away.

in and out

Pavilion,
Heinerscheid
Light Bar,
Luxembourg

Architect
n-lab architects, 2006
Steinmetz De Meyer
architectes urbanistes,
2003

pavilions

This wooden pavilion in Heinerscheid stands next to the main building like an over-dimensional piece of garden furniture. Its main function is protection from wind and weather.
Directed towards the east and with single glazing, the barely thirty-square-metre interior is warmed by the morning sun. This means that there is also an agreeable indoor climate during autumn and winter. The sun-protection made of aluminium rods can be manually adjusted to any position according to the sun's radiation. The prefabricated structure and details reduced to a minimum made it possible to realise the pavilion economically – without sacrificing the Retro-Pop-Design.

The Light Bar pavilion belongs to an entire complex of entertainment buildings already planned during the early 1990s in Luxembourg-Hollerich. The individual buildings, grouped around an inner courtyard, are now joined together by the long extended, narrow bar. Its curved roof is not only an eye-catcher, but also an essential component of its spatial staging; in the summer, the light construction of steel and glass opens up to the courtyard – bar and terrace then form a unity.
In the winter, the entrances are on each end of the façade; large sliding shutters of steel and wooden laths in the middle area of the glass façade serve as an atmospheric filter between interior and exterior, lending the interior a warm atmosphere.
The gravitation point of the 100-square-metre bar is the nine-metre-long counter made of brushed stainless-steel plates (which almost appear to be folded) in front of a turquoise-colour background accentuating the length of the room.
Special attention has been directed to the lighting effects. The lighting is concentrated on the illumination of innumerable glass bottles in the niches of the turquoise-coloured wall and of the glasses on the counter. Thanks to the multi-coloured lighting concept, the lighting dramaturgy is able to follow the changing moods in the room.

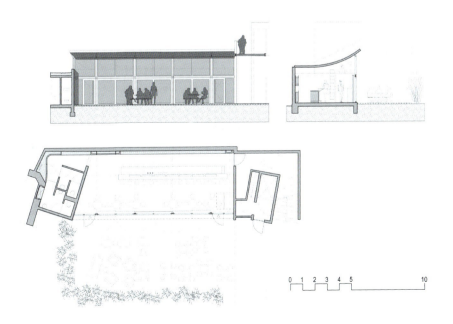

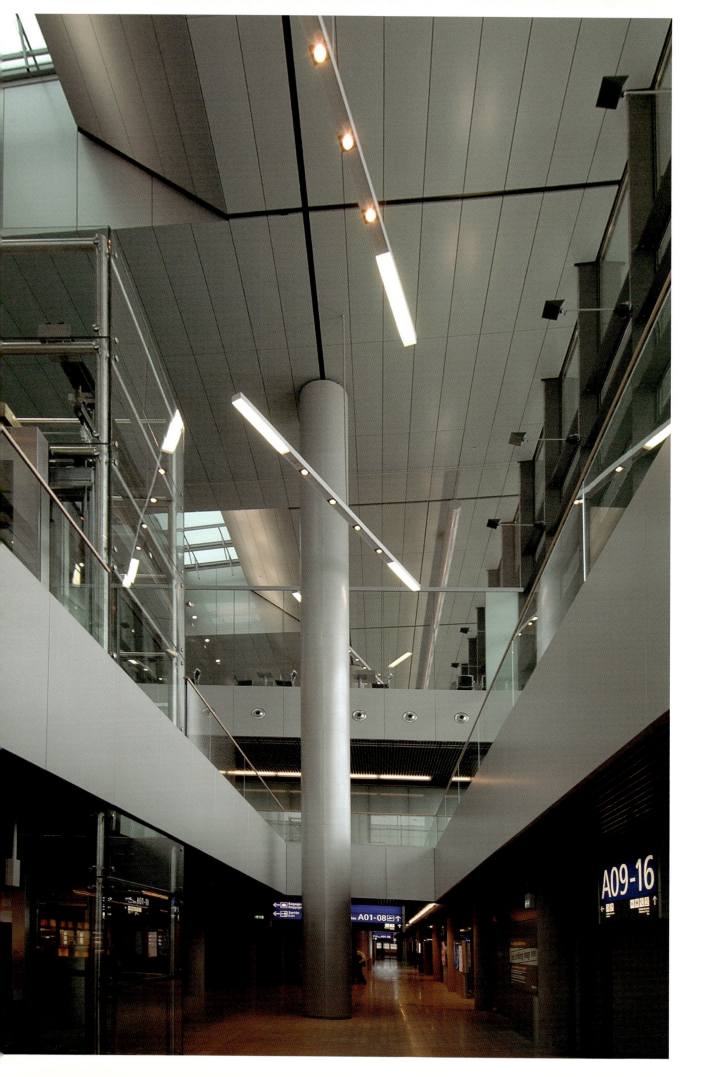

libre circulation

New Building Terminal A at Luxembourg Airport

Architect
Paczowski et Fritsch
Architectes, 2008

infrastructure

The new terminal with its clear geometrical lines is modelled closely on the old building, a fact also reflected in its architecture. The new building is not only the prestigious gateway to Luxembourg for visitors arriving by air; it is also an extremely modern and efficient facility for the processing of passengers and freight and complies with all the high security standards expected of an international airport. Writing in 1946, Le Corbusier was of the opinion that "an airport should be naked, naked under the heavens, naked before the fields and runways." The architecture of the building reflects this ethos, its angular geometric form in stark contrast to the aerodynamic lines of the aircraft.

The planners opted for simple, even minimalist shapes and materials – glass surfaces, granite floors, walls of metal, wood and exposed concrete. With its clarity of form the building makes a simple and direct statement. It was conceived as a covered complex, the roof being a full 10,000 square metres in area. This roof with its southerly overhang is the building's chief architectural feature. It shields the interior from excessive sunlight and, on the other side of the terminal, the overhang protects passengers arriving by car or bus from rain as they make their way to the airport building. Systematically arranged domed skylights illuminate the entire concourse with natural light. The various levels are connected via staircases, escalators, lifts and moving walkways. The natural ten-metre height differential between the covered forecourt and the airfield allows groups of passengers to be steered and partitioned off from each other as required by the security authorities. Nonetheless all terminal users have access to the panorama restaurant on the upper floor.

On entering the terminal passengers find themselves on the open concourse with its shops, lounges, 26 check-in desks and security checking area for departing passengers. On the upper level the restaurant offers a clear view across the runways to the open countryside and woods in the distance. The northern side of the lower level provides access to trains and the underground parking. This is also the location of the arrivals hall and the baggage claims area. On the other side, facing the runways, are the departure halls and five telescoping access passageways. A special terminal has been built for small-aircraft traffic, which represents a major part of flights into and out of Luxembourg. The terminal is connected to the main building by a 200 metre long passage and is completely glazed on the east side; its western façade protects the hall from strong sunlight. From a spacious waiting room with VIP lounge and bar passengers use one of ten exits as they walk to the aircraft parked around the terminal. Arriving passengers enter the building via one of six exterior staircases or escalators evenly distributed along the terminal. The terminal's ceiling and the interior wall on the west side are covered in wooden cladding, the entire area exuding warmth and solidity.

❮ The anatomy of an airport: views of the terminal building

↑ Model view, longitudinal section

cogeneration

infrastructure

Block-Type Thermal Power Station, Luxembourg-Kirchberg

Architect
Paul Bretz Architectes, 2001

A block heat and power station with administration building has been constructed in an exposed position on the Kirchberg plateau to provide power for the town's new district. Architect and engineer collaborated to produce a compact, exposed-concrete building whose fundamental design is a direct reflection of the power station's function.

The station is composed of four sections directly facing the road. A three-storey administration building and three-storey heat storage facility abut these sections at their respective ends. Each thermal power section has its own chimney, boiler and engine room. Glass slits divide the sections one from another, allowing natural light to enter and providing an interesting glimpse into the interior workings of a power station.

The building blends with remarkable harmony into the flanking buildings of a major road without diminishing in any way the impression of concision and compactness that it itself gives. The Luxembourg power company also decided to move its head offices here. It was not only this unusual combination of office and plant that proved a challenge to architects and engineers; the conspicuous location of the complex also posed issues that had to be solved. The project demanded that an office building in combination with a purely functional, technically complex and essentially bulky industrial plant be harmoniously inserted into an urban setting. That the architects succeeded in reconciling all these functions in what appears to be a mono-functional building can be attributed to their close working relationship with the construction company, since three storeys is an unconventional height for large block-type thermal power stations. At closer inspection, however, the building discloses its different functions. The four high chimneys at the centre of the complex provide the clearest clue to the building's use. The symbolism of the soaring towers is accentuated by the optical partitioning off of the production facilities. This alternation between walls and glass slits is contained at the left end by the hermetically sealed block with its water storage tanks reaching deep down into the ground and on the right by the admin building with its all-glass frontage. This glazed façade signals a change of function yet the building's concrete framework clearly identifies the administration block as an integral part of the whole complex.

› The battery of the four chimneys adds rhythm to the Boulevard

The beauty of austerity: unusually precious materials determine the inside rooms

max 0.33 herz

Radar Tower, Luxembourg Findel

Architect
Atelier d'Architecture & de Design Jim Clemes, 2006

infrastructuro

The Findel Airport required a new radar tower with a dome, the so-called Radom. Since the tower had to project above the planned maintenance hangar for wide-bodied aircraft, it came about that the tower reached a height of 43.50 metres without the dome. The operations were also to include a transformer station and a spare-parts depot. While the radar control room had to stand in direct contact to the radar, the other functional rooms were to be arranged at ground level.

The architects wanted to give the purely technical building an autonomous aesthetic quality, so they limited themselves to the use of concrete and glass. Exposed concrete not only offered the statically necessary rigidity, but also a sophisticated appearance and a high surface quality. The tower itself is a plate construction. Two of these plates thrust out three metres from the square ground-plan resulting from two cubes, thus giving the tower a clear orientation in the direction of the airfield. The third plate forms the spine, serving to brace the entire construction.

The entrance, transformer station and spare-parts depot are located in the ground-level cube. The second cube houses the radar control room and is 37.50 metres high. The Radom, with a diameter of 14 metres, is placed upon it; ultimately, it is nothing more than a protective sheath around the permanently turning radar. The roof of the control level is accessible from every direction for maintenance purposes. The vertical connection of the two spatial volumes has been provided with a stairway and a lift embedded between the two protruding plates.

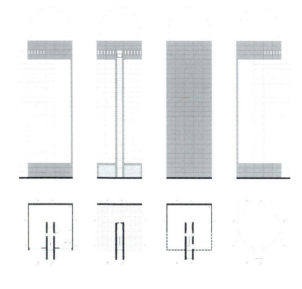

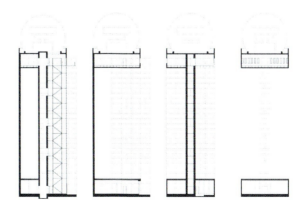

water cone

infrastructure

Reservoir, Hivange

Architect
Georges Reuter
Architectes,
Schroeder & Associés,
2002

Hivange in the district of Garnich is the site of a new water tower and reservoir built by the Syndicat des Eaux du Sud Koerich. The installation occupies a rural setting featuring traditional village architecture. The spectacular 31-metre-high conical tower is reminiscent of a Scythian burial mound, a kurgan from the steppes of southern Russia or an Egyptian pyramid. The pointed structure, clad in aluminium, stands in direct contrast to the rural area.

Form and building materials seem at first glance to be quiet alien to the surroundings, the edifice appearing as a huge symbol or weighty hieroglyphic. Yet the architects devoted much energy to achieving harmony with the surroundings without compromising on modernity.

The installation consists of two sections – tower and attached building. They are covered with grass and together give the appearance of a natural elevation, with the concrete structure and equipment concealed from view. The base of the installation communicates solidity and a link with the ground while the conical upper part points to the horizon. The installation presents a successful symbiosis of sky and earth and can be compared to a sacred building in its form and presence. Form here is not to be taken as representing an alien cultural characteristic or decorative style to be considered in its historical context but rather as a continuation of the notion that architecture can regenerate itself using geometrical structures.

viaduct

infrastructure

Route du Nord, Viaduc de Lorentzweiler

Architect
Bureau d'Architecture & de Design Jim Clemes, 2006

In an elegant leap this slender yet solid bridge spans the railway line and Alzette valley near Lintgen. If designed sensitively a bridge can remove from a motorway the stigma often attached to a ribbon of concrete carving through the countryside. Aware of the effect that a bridge of this size might have on an otherwise undisturbed landscape the architects directed their efforts towards achieving full integration and harmony with nature.

The choice of local building materials, dry stone walls, local vegetation and the landscaping of the soil have produced a building of black concrete fully integrated into the valley's physiognomy. Concrete was used to blend the bridge's form with its dynamic distribution of forces. Special attention was paid to the elements connecting bridge and tunnel. The architectural style of these works of art marks the completion of the topographical sectioning that began at the entrances to the Gousselerbierg Tunnel.

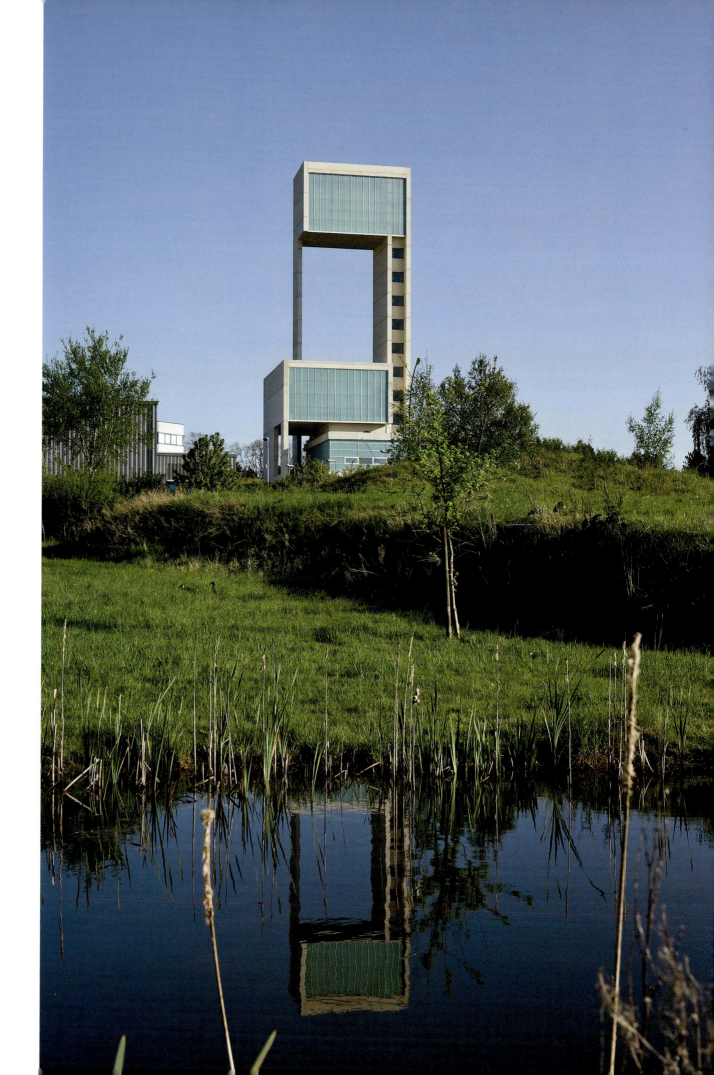

potential

Reservoir / Technical Services and Fire Department, Leudelange

Architect
SchemelWirtz architectes, 2007

infrastructure

The design was informed by the topography of the area and the role of the installation. The laws of physics required that the first water tank, with a water capacity of 500 cubic metres, be located 45 metres above the ground. A second container, holding up to 900 cubic metres, is fixed at an elevation of eleven metres.
Due to the sloping ground the fire engines use two separate approach roads to access the Leudelange District's equipment and maintenance shed, the workshop and another hangar. The complex cluster of exposed concrete cubes is visible at a great distance. The night illuminations underscore the interplay of concrete and back-lit glass surfaces.

↑ The complex cluster of exposed concrete cubes is visible at a great distance

homage

Emile Mayrisch Monument, Esch-sur-Alzette

Architect
Auguste and Gustave Perret, 1933

patrimony

"An absurd accident, a burst tyre!, and at 130 km/hr. What hope is there of stopping a three thousand kilo vehicle heading for a tree at breakneck speed. I rage and rage at this kind of avoidable disaster. He was on the way to Paris, and seven kilometres beyond Châlons he was killed in a car crash …" Thus wrote Maria van Rysselberghe on 21st May 1928 in a letter to Jean Schlumberger.

Emile Mayrisch Square in Esch-sur-Alzette was inaugurated in 1929. As early as 1926 Hermann Josef Stübben had submitted his draft for a square near Dellheicht School as part of his designs for the town of Esch. Auguste and Gustave Perret put forward two designs for an Emile Mayrisch monument to be erected on this verdant island. The eventual monument took the form of a rectangular column incorporated into the plinth by means of a 54 x 54 centimetres, slightly tapering lower section. The 70 centimetre high bust at the top of the column is the work of the sculptor Louis Dejean (1872–1952), who also created the two bronze reliefs on both sides of the column. The reliefs depict two scenes from the world of heavy industry and were cast by the Parisian Ferdinand Barbedienne.

The Perret brothers also produced the designs for Emile Mayrisch's grave in Colpach (1928) and the monument in Châlons-sur-Marne (1930), where Emile Mayrisch lost his life. The monument to the industrialist and philanthropist in Esch was unveiled on 15th August 1933.

pont

The Red Bridge, Luxembourg

Architect
Egon Jux, 1965

Project
Paolo Soleri, 1958

patrimony

The Grande Duchesse Charlotte Bridge, otherwise known as Roud Bréck or the Red Bridge, links the upper part of Luxembourg City to the European District on the Kirchberg. At the time of its construction in 1960–1965, based on a design by architect Egon Jux, anti-rust paint was only available in red. Nobody wants to be held responsible for the choice of colour during the long history of the bridge, although hardly any other colour would have suited this construction and the valley. 68 designs were submitted in response to the 1957 tendering of this project to span the valley of the Alzette. They ranged from reinforced concrete girder bridges and arched bridges and truss constructions to steel beam or steel arch bridges and suspension bridges. The jury of experts proposed to their client, the Luxembourg government, the construction of a steel truss bridge designed by the Rheinstahl Union Brückenbau group from Dortmund under Socol Bruxelles and Jean Think from Differdange. The final construction differed only slightly from the original design; one change involved the engineers' decision to use screwed joints instead of rivets.

The Red Bridge spans the district of Pfaffenthal at a height of 74 metres. 25 metres wide and weighing over 4,900 tons the bridge is 355 metres long and has a bearing distance of 234 metres. As the bridge came to be used by people to commit suicide from a Plexiglass wall was installed in 1990.

"Le pont rouge," a short film directed by Geneviève Mersch in 1991, documents the experiences of the Pfaffenthals inhabitants whose houses lie directly beneath the bridge.

This bright red, modern bridge stands as a symbol of the revival of Luxembourg's urban development in the decades after the Second World War.

Paolo Soleri suggested alternative projects for this competition. They have so far remained unknown.
left/above: Levitation Bridge
following pages: Omega Bridge, Balance Bridge, Campanula Bridge, Flight Bridge, Helium Bridge, Spanning Bridge

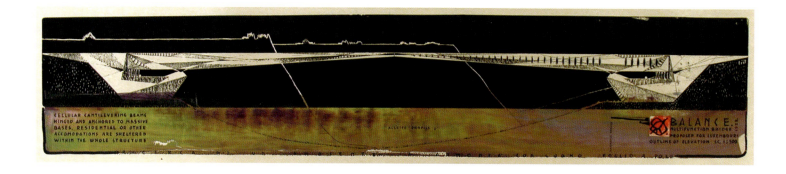

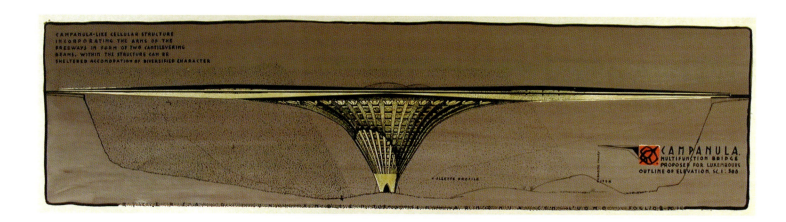

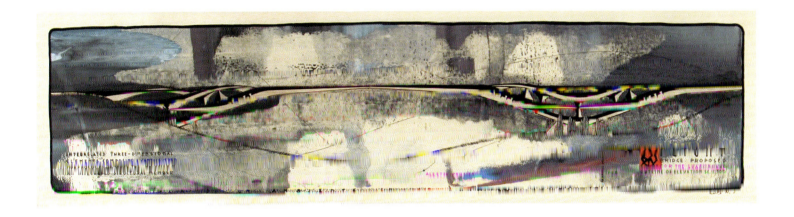
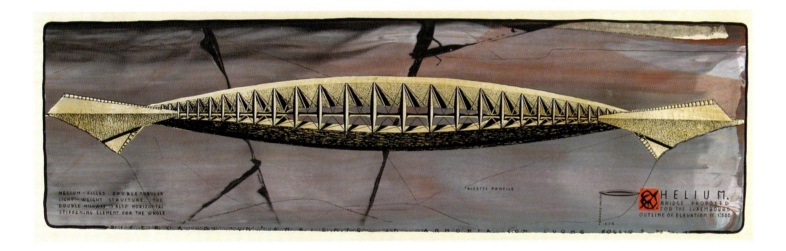

01 02

03

reflection

334 **constructive** emmanuel j. petit

Pieter Brueghel the Elder:
The Tower of Babel, 1563

constructive

reflection

Emmanuel J. Petit

The artistic avantgarde deviates always from the institutional status quo of the era. If we accept the zeitgeist argument of architectural modernism, the avantgarde architect is successful in expressing the fundamental yet hidden energy of his era. In this process existing forms are challenged and replaced by those which are novel. Because the avantgarde always wishes to be the forerunner, it has paradoxically a history of its own, the tradition of thinking in negatives. In this manner institutions are destroyed, to be replaced by new ones. This structural dialectic between the destruction of existing institutions and the construction of new forms underlies each avantgarde.

The institution of the museum has a particularly ambivalent relationship to the avantgarde. As an "institution of conservation" the museum is subject, on the one hand, to the avantgarde's criticism and, on the other, dependent on the latter's intellectual innovations for the purposes of fulfilling its cultural task. As a result, production of an architectural design for a museum is itself an interesting challenge. In realising that task, architecture advances to become the self-conscious symptom of this ambivalence, as will be discussed here in the light of three examples: the Centre Pompidou in Paris by Renzo Piano and Richard Rogers, the Abteiberg Museum by Hans Hollein in Mönchengladbach, and the Museum of Modern Art (MUDAM) by Ieoh Ming Pei in Luxembourg.

Negation has been at times a highly effective strategy with which to the challenge the status quo of an era. It may be recalled, for example, how the surrealists rejected traditional concepts of reality, or how the nihilistic statements of dadaism shattered the existing understanding of meaning. The death of art has been repeatedly announced, as for example in Tatlin's verdict: "Art is dead! Long live the new machine art!" withdrawing history and tradition from the realms of art. In that situation, the ruinous state of traditional thinking advances to an iconoclastic spectacle, and the "creation" of the new form becomes a quasi-romantic drama. In this context the drama develops from the fact that the result produced by human hand can ever only constitute a fragment of an infinite creative potential extending beyond the scope of complete depiction. It is possible only to express that which is broken, inadequate, shattered and alienating. Consider, for example, the landscape painting of the romantic artist, Friedrich Gilly, in which the subject gazes with existential profundity into the depths of an infinite landscape disappearing within the mists.

The unfamiliar is confronted with our yearning for the familiar, that is to say the status quo. Wherever the unfamiliar is perceived by our senses as impressive and overpowering, the aesthetic category of the sublime is called into play. According to Immanuel Kant, we call sublime "what is absolutely large" – and as result we can perceive only ever a fragment of the grand creative idea – and that "… the sublime is what pleases immediately by reason of its opposition to the interest of sense" ("… was durch seinen Widerstand gegen das Interesse der Sinne unmittelbar gefällt," *Kritik der Urteilskraft*, 1790). When confronted with the sublime, the senses are overtaxed, overwhelmed, and seemingly tricked since the unfamiliar reveals to them, nonetheless, the presence of beauty. Language has taken account of this paradox in expressions such as "frightfully beautiful" or "terribly beautiful". Accordingly, certain things can in moral terms be terrible and yet enchant our senses. A further example can be found in the artificial, ruinous follies of romantic landscape gardens whose aesthetic charms derive from a wrecked past, as may be seen in the Roman ruins contained in the gardens of Vienna's Schönbrunn Palace.

The architecture of the 1980s revitalised similarly romantic themes, for example, in architectural deconstruction in which the ruined Tower of Babel became a controversial icon. The ruined tower demonstrates the both fatal and dramatic impossibility of a coherent architectural form – the Hebrew word for Babel "bilbul" means confusion. In 1988 the expression "Deconstructive Architecture" was coined as the title of an exhibition held at New York's Museum of Modern Art (MOMA). That phrase was, in turn, expression of the existential doubts held by its protagonists. Frank O. Gehry, Rem Koolhaas, Zaha Hadid, Günther Behnisch, Coop Himmelb(l)au, Peter Eisenman, and Bernard Tschumi: once, the leaders of a destructive attack on the architectural institution, in the meantime they have become the institution itself. Their thinking in negatives produced a positive contribution to architecture. Since the form paradigms advanced in their architecture have been absorbed in the meantime within construction, architecture is called upon to search for new methods by which form may be generated and established.

Again, the historical dialetic of the avantgarde – identified by the Marxist architectural theorist, Manfredo Tafuri, in texts such as *Progetto e utopia* and *Sfera e il labirinto* – can be observed. The institutional reality of architecture transforms each negative and critical thought inevitably to become a "constructive" contribution. Through architecture negative thought is transformed into a positive production. Construction – inherent in all architecture – can never be negative. It is the epitome always of the positive and the constitutive. This conceptual aporia demands that architecture develop its own epistomology rather than adopt in uncritical fashion that which attaches to other disciplines or to its own tradition. Architecture constitutes both thoughts on form and is itself a form of thought. Where a failure to take seriously that irony arises, architecture becomes parody or kitsch, since institutional rituals are aped in platitudes.

Whilst in their self-referential emphasis on the impossibility of formal integrity the deconstructionists sought to settle accounts with architectural expressionism, the postmodernists began to play with the citation of part actual and part fictional history. Harnessing the techniques of collage and montage, postmodernism created buildings and cities in the same way as a carpet is woven – providing a parodical account of the Garden of Eden or the legendary Atlantis. Familiar to us as an example of that ideological approach is Luxembourg's Cité Judiciaire currently under construction on the Saint-Esprit plateau. The myth surrounding Arcadia, Atlantis or the Golden Age is portrayed as an inalterable and unchallengeable constant, as, for example, in Léon Krier's Atlantis project. From the perspective of that intellectual approach, seeking its salvation in the starting point of all culture, any orientation towards the future or utopia appears suspect, nihilistic and negative. Instead, the dream of Arcadia endows a validity to the forms and institutional practices of architecture: a pediment is a pediment, a triglyph is a triglyph, and a balustrade is a balustrade.

Notwithstanding the many differences between deconstructionism and postmodernism both approaches adopt a critical stance to the architecture of modernism. Thus, it appears sensible at this point to cast a look back to the 1950s, a period in which a young generation of architects redefined the classical modernism of Mies van der Rohe, Walter Gropius or Le Corbusier. Following the dictum of Mies that "form follows function" and Le Corbusier's definition of a house as a *machine à habiter*, modernism experienced a redefinition through the work of architects such as Eero Saarinen, Louis Kahn,

Philip Johnson, or Ieoh Ming Pei. This generation reworked the functional, organisational foundations of modernism, endowing them with an aesthetically formal character or extending them to include a metaphorical dimension. Whereas classical modernism wished to be abstract, namely not "to say" anything, merely "to be", in his design for the TWA Terminal at New York's JFK Airport Eero Saarinen proposed a building which with its daring pre-stressed concrete roof was undoubtedly modern but also metaphorical. The roof alluded to the wings of a bird, rather than reveal functional and technical facets of the building's interior. The building speaks to the function of flight. Le Corbusier's comparison of a building to a machine is replaced by the semantic dimension of form. Henceforth, a building must not merely function, but it must somehow also identify and communicate the idea underlying its function.

Louis I. Kahn's designs are, on the contrary, self-referential geometrical forms. In these works, modernism's preference for asymmetry experiences a return to more formal patterns. Kahn reflects his forms in a classical manner, with the resulting symmetries creating hermetic references, which independent of urban context or functional relationships in the building's interior space give rise to hermetic "meaning".

Many of his designs exhibit ground plans shaped in crystal-like forms. Noticeable in these compositions is the use of the 45 degree angle and the diagonal. In actual fact, almost all of Kahn's compositions are based on the square, the diamond and the circle. The diagonal plays a major role also in Philip Johnson's architecture from this period, for example in his Pennzoil Towers in Houston, Texas, where two diagonally angled-off towers produce a jagged skyline and, in addition, are located on a pyramid-shaped base. The 45 degree angle can be described as an invention of the architecture of the 1950s. Buckminster Fuller was another architect to adopt this vocabulary of form in the shape of his geodesic domes. He used the 45 degree angle less as a formalistic but as a tectonic instrument. For example, in 1967 for the Montreal Expo he erected a spherical triangulated structure assembled from pyramid-shaped details.

In the 1960s Ieoh Ming Pei began to use also large-scale forms as a criticism of the classical, white, functional and dematerialised forms of modernism. He acquired great renown with his winning entry in the competition for the John F. Kennedy Library in Boston (1964–79). The design went through various stages, all of which, however, are based on the same formal principles: the introduction of the diagonal, allowing for triangular and pyramid-shaped forms and volumes, and calling into question the modernist insistence on right-angles. The original 1964 design, which without a doubt brings to mind Luxembourg's Museum of Modern Art, constructed some forty years later, comprises a stone cuboid together with an angled-off glass pyramid, enclosing a large entrance hall. In those days, criticism was expressed at the selection of a young architect who questioned the canon of modernism with his unusual forms based on Platonic solids.

Pei was avantgarde – although not in the Marxist sense. Pei and his contemporaries had defined a new architecture, distinguished through its formalisation of large-scale squares or circles implemented in ambitious steel and glass constructions and its use of diagonal – not frontal – alignment. These ideas characterise an entire series of his

↑ Bank of China Tower, Hong Kong
architect: I. M. Pei

❰ TransWorldAirlines Terminal, New York, architect: Eero Saarinen

Bangladesh Parliament, Dhaka, architect: Louis I. Kahn

buildings: John Hancock Tower in Boston (1966–76) is a prismatic glass structure with a ground plan which is not right-angled but based on a parallelogram; the Municipal Administration Center in Dallas, where a concrete façade adapted from Le Corbusier leans outwards along the building's entire length (1966–77); and finally the never-built Helix Tower which construction magnate William Zeckendorf wanted to erect on the banks of New York's East River. Whilst this vocabulary of forms was an invention of the 1950s and 1960s avantgarde, nonetheless, Pei recycled it in the 1980s in his pyramid for the Louvre in Paris.

The formal clarity and the iconographic brevity of their architecture helped this genre also to achieve major commercial success. The large-scale forms could easily be employed as the emblems of firms and multi-nationals. They were a prestigious and highly flexible framework with which to organise the building's variable inner workings. With Zeckendorf's assistance as an investor, Pei developed to become a highly recognised corporate architect. This image runs as a constant through his career. Namely, some fifteen years ago he designed a fantastic skyscraper for the Bank of China in Hong Kong, without a doubt a considerable reinforcement to the bank's corporate identity. Despite the formal elegance of that building, Pei's play on the triangle in its façade and structure was, however, at this stage no longer avantgarde.

The formal clarity mentioned immediately above and the conceptual narrow-mindedness of such architecture have become since the 1960s increasingly the focus for criticism. The potential with regard to form contained within that strategy began to repeat itself and thus advanced to become the status quo and not the critical exception. More and more prismatic and mirrored structures began to adorn the outskirts of cities and industrial estates. A brief sketch may explain how between the 1960s and 1970s architectural discourse then came to experience a thematic shift. An important method by which formal limitations were challenged lay in the "diagrammatic processes", which emerged in the architecture of the 1960s as a critique of late modernism.

Two very different diagrammatic approaches may be identified – one organisational, the other formalistic. The Centre Pompidou and the Abteiberg Museum may be regarded as flagships of each of the respective approaches.

First, the organisational diagram. In 1965 the British architectural theorist Reyner Banham published a text entitled *A Home is not a House*, in which he wrote, "When your house contains such a complex of piping, flues, ducts, wires, lights, inlets, outlets, ovens, sinks, refuse disposers, hi-fi reverberators, antennae, conduits, freezers, heaters – when it contains so many services that the hardware could stand up by itself without any assistance from the house, why have a house to hold it up?" Where buildings contain an ever increasing number of technical fittings, why should these be hidden behind plasterwork, false floors and ceilings? Why should this reality of a building not be made visible or even elevated to the structure of the house itself? Banham's suggestion generates a whole new basis on which to discuss questions of architectural form. In this context, traditional categories of regulating architectural form – such as proportion, articulation of structure, or symmetry – are rendered obsolete. During the modernist period a transformation in the "anatomy of living" (Banham's title for the illustration accompanying his text) occurred. Henceforth, the architect needs no longer design a house's form, rather its form results primarily from technical requirements. Should a house require in addition to its technical fittings the presence of a climatic envelope, a highly flexible and amorphous skin may be stretched around the technical elements to create a sealed "climatic bubble". This takes Le Corbusier's concept of a *machine à habiter* to extremes, but aesthetic expression is less important here than the new social reality which may potentially emerge.

What are the features of this changed social reality? In the circles of the British "independent group", to which, in addition to Banham, architects such as Alice and Peter Smithson, the Archigram Group, and Cedric Price also belonged, technoid architectural designs were presented alongside a new social programme. Archigram advanced proposals for utopias in which, for example, entire districts could be moved on telescopic legs in the search for new social neighbourhoods or to meet new challenges with regard to mobility, as for example in Ron Herron's 1964 design for a "Walking City". Anyone doubting the feasibility of such a utopia should compare the scale of that project with the liner Queen Mary 2. This ship travels backwards and forwards like a small town plying the journey between Europe and the United States. Moreover, dreams already exist for floating cities such as the floating continent "Freedom – City at Sea", where a permanent residence – and thereby the benefits of certain tax advantages – can be acquired. Although these examples are merely capitalistic perversions of Archigram's social utopias they are all the same fed by similar technoid visions of utopia.

A further example can be found in Cedric Price's "fun palace", a project which he designed for London in the early 1960s. The building comprises merely the technical infrastructure needed for entertainment purposes. Stages, loudspeakers, monitors and audience seating can be moved around freely within its steel frame. A "form" in a classical sense could not be identified in this building: the 1960s was a period in which recognisability of form was readily equated with a symptom of social control exerted by the ruling classes over the oppressed. Naturally, this building cannot escape its origins as a contemporary of the hippie generation, which held form – and the institution of architecture – in explicit contempt. No longer was architecture to attest to the dusty and academic rigour of the academies – which at the time continued to be concerned with questions regarding the compositional reference generated by the square, circle or diagonal – instead, architecture was to be placed unconditionally at the service of living. The prevailing sentiment was: "life's already a chaos – let architecture do the same". Underscoring further this notion of provisionality, on the title page of his latest book Cedric Price writes: "Best before 1st May 2006. By that date the author may have changed his mind."

In 1971 the competition for the Centre Pompidou Museum is won by two young architects, Richard Rogers and Renzo Piano. Following their graduation in architecture, this building was their first project and through their efforts the technoid utopia mentioned immediately above acquires a specific form. In the journal *L'architecture*

> Louvre Pyramid, Paris,
architect: I. M. Pei

d'aujourd'hui Maurice Culot – a Marxist champion of Léon Krier – published a counter-proposal, in which in a reactionary step he placed the steel pipes and ducting where they traditionally belong: behind a façade. That suggestion was intended to render the winning design a farce. However, the suggestion itself turned out to be ridiculous. Piano and Rogers prevailed with their vision, designating the technical fittings as the façade. The design for the Centre Pompidou is the tip of an iceberg of architectural discussion, making this building of the most important institutions of the 20th century. The Centre Pompidou and the exhibitions it houses are characterised primarily in terms of the building and its architecture and only at a secondary level by the curatorial efforts within its walls. The Centre Pompidou characterised like virtually no other building the understanding of architecture and art in the 1970s, endowing art with a new status in the social sphere.

One of the most provocative postmodern theorists, Jean Baudrillard, coined the phrase "Beaubourg effect" (*L'effet beaubourg, Implosion et dissuasion,* 1977). According to him, for the first time in history a museum is not viewed as a bastion of art, rather this building provokes French culture to "implode". As a consequence of this effect of implosion Jean Baudrillard labels the Centre Beaubourg, Les Halles and the Park de la Villette advertising monuments (or anti-monuments), because from the outset these were meant to be a demonstration of the operation of culture, of the cultural operation of commodity and the masses in movement. At these sites traditional distinctions between culture and consumption implode, the museum sucks the masses literally into its inner space. Suddenly, the crate surrounding the museum – its architecture – is more modern than the modern art which is on display within. The crate attracts the masses "… not because they salivate for that culture which they have been denied for centuries, but because they have for the first time the opportunity to massively participate in this great mourning of a culture that, in the end, they have always detested."

Whatever the changes in the cultural landscape and cultural audience which ensued, the starting point for this hedonistic and technoid revolution was architecture. Responsibility for the Centre Pompidou's transformation as a visible institution was to be found in its radical and self-confident aura. Inside, however, the pictures on view were the same Picasso, the same Rothko or Miró, the same Arp and Léger, as could be viewed also in New York, Venice, Berlin or Tokyo. Nonetheless, this building existed only in the Paris which dared to be avantgarde. In addition to this example – which in its critique of Platonistic modernism derives from the organisational diagram – regard must be had also to the formalistic diagram. In the late 1960s, the latter genre of diagram, too, was intended as a critique of the formal clarity and monumentalism of the generation characterised by Saarinen, Johnson, Kahn, and Pei.

In the early 1960s the architectural theorist Colin Rowe and the painter Robert Slutzky wrote a influential text *Transparency: Literal and Phenomenal*, in which they oppose the modernist canon of formal clarity and advocate a complex language of form in architecture. In that article they investigate the phenomenon of "transparency", according to which a visual surface not only contains information on the forms ordered therein but also reveals structural and spatial connections to figures behind. Thus, transparency must be understood in a broader sense. Transparency is not simply the property of a material permitting a view to penetrate in a literal sense but generates a kind of double entendre. Phenomenal transparency requires intellectual decoding, since it hints merely at the surface of hidden forms. This cubist version of architecture opens up the possibility to display simultaneously various spatial layers on the same visual surface, for example, a façade .

In his book *Collage City* (1978) Colin Rowe extended his theory of formal complexity to the sphere of urban planning. According to that view, the city is not a formal continuum, but a collage of differing perspectives and, consequently, diverse geometries. Leaving aside such utopian creations as Brasilia or Palmanova cities are a combination of diverse utopias. The city magma consists of many individual utopian islands which together produce a quasi-chaotic, complex unity. Rowe draws on Karl Popper's social philosophy, in which Popper emphasises the reality of differing points of view bearing "pocket waistcoat utopias" in collision with one another. Just as ethics and epistemology had to adapt to this new consciousness of relativity, urban planning, too, reacted with the development of new theories. Rowe describes how neighbouring small utopias within the city have to hold formal "negotiations" with one another concerning their boundaries and that in such a process an interesting bounded area (poché) may arise. The ground plan of the Emperor Hadrian's villa was advanced as an icon of this collage style of urban development. Partly by reason of the site's topography, but also on account of aesthetic considerations, the villa was divided amongst various structures which refer to one another in a diversity of angles.

In 1972, more or less at the same time as the Centre Pompidou development, Hans Hollein begins in Mönchengladbach to plan the Abteiberg Museum. One of his sketches reveals how here, too, wildly differing geometrical forms are cast together to create a complex bounded space – namely, urban space – similar to that found at Hadrian's villa. A cylinder, a chequerboard, an undulated form, a tower and a ruptured form are brought together no longer to define a building as a self-contained object but as if it were a small town. A diversity of external and internal spaces exists, seemingly brought together in a random collage, a kind of architectural cubism, decisively calling into question the ideology of large-scale forms of the 1950s. The Abteiberg Museum was a pathbreaking development. Its construction brought about a transformation to an entire series of German museums. Not least James Stirling's Staatsgalerie in Stuttgart and the museums along Frankfurt's museum mile were buildings to make a habit out of this collage principle. The idea that a building is not a self-contained object fixed to the ground, but that a building can be terrain, topography and structure at the same time has transformed in turn understandings of architecture, cities and art.

Ieoh Ming Pei's museum in Luxembourg makes no claim to avantgarde status. In terms of ideology it should be evident from the foregoing observations where this building has to be placed. When Paris chose Pei in the early 1980s for the remodelling of the Louvre, a debate took place at least on the treatment of historic buildings, although even at that stage a glass pyramid no longer could be described as avantgarde. Pei's pyramid prompted a debate which helped Europeans

free themselves somewhat from their debilitating and conservative attitudes to the conservation of historic buildings. However, as regards the Luxembourg museum, a biographer of the architect told me in relation to that building that Pei had said: "Oh, Luxembourg was interested in the Mitterrand effect." Following the "Beaubourg effect" of the Centre Pompidou and the "Bilbao effect" which Frank O. Gehry's Guggenheim Museum in the Basque city is reputed to have produced, what in terms of architectural history might be meant by the "Mitterrand effect"?

It is the notion that a building such as the Pyramid at the Louvre can in fact lend expression to an era, to a city, to a nation and to art. Where a building achieves that objective, architecture transforms itself to become architecture pointing beyond the construction of more or less well-designed buildings. Only sometimes does that architecture give birth to an icon which embodies new ideas. The Centre Pompidou and the Abteiberg Museum pursued their cultural task seriously and accordingly came to be regarded as milestones in architectural history and as cultural and political statements of their period. Without a doubt they owe this honour to their avantgarde position. Namely, only something which remains free of a howsoever codified meaning has the capacity to become the icon of a new era.

04

appendix

345 **biographies**
347 **credits**

biographies

ulf meyer

Ulf Meyer studied architecture at the Technische Universität, Berlin, and the Illinois Institute of Technology in Chicago. Since 1996 freelance writer and journalist for architecture and urban planning in Berlin. Numerous publications in newspapers, journals and books in Germany and abroad. 2000/2001: Nippon-Carl-Duisberg-Gesellschaft (NCDG) stipendiary at Shigeru Ban Architects in Tokyo/Japan. 2004: Working stay at Berkeley/California as guest editor on San Francisco Chronicle, sponsored by Arthur F. Burns Fellowship for journalists. Since 2008 professor of architecture and environmentally friendly urban planning at Kansas State University/USA.

alain linster

Alain Linster studied architecture in Innsbruck and under Hans Hollein at the Summer Academy in Salzburg. Project work for Josef Paul Kleihues. Ateliers Flammang and Linster in Esch-sur-Alzette and Münster. Since 2000 in partnership with Jos Dell and Marie Lucas at m3 architectes. Projects: renovation of CFL Luxembourg, European Court of Justice (with Dominique Perrault, Paczowski et Fritsch), Theatre National Luxembourg, Rehazenter Luxembourg-Kirchberg and others. Numerous publications in Almanach 2000, l'Art au Luxembourg Fonds Mercator 2006, Fondation de l'Architecture et de l'Ingénierie series on Luxembourg architects.

credits

introduction

1, 5 "La Porte," architect: Ricardo Bofill © Marco Kany, www.letoile.eu   7 architect: Atelier d'Architecture & de Design Jim Clemes © G. G. Kirchner   10 architect: Paul Bretz Architectes © CNA, Romain Girtgen   11 architect: Christian Bauer © Lukas Roth, www.lukas-roth.com   14 architect: Bruck + Weckerle Architekten © Lukas Roth, www.lukas-roth.com   16 architect: Atelier d'Architecture & de Design Jim Clemes © Willi Filz   20, 22–25 © Marco Kany, www.letoile.eu

culture

28 MUDAM, Luxembourg
28 © Marco Kany, www.letoile.eu   30 © Musée d'Art Moderne Grand-Duc Jean, MUDAM Luxembourg, André Weisgerber   30 artwork: © Fernando Sánchez Castillo, Nous sommes tous indésirables, 2006   31, 32 View of the Gaylen Gerber exhibition with e. a. Joe Scanlan's Pay Dirt (2003) from MUDAM's collection, photo: Rémi Villaggi   33 © Musée d'Art Moderne Grand-Duc Jean, MUDAM Luxembourg, Christian Aschman   33 artwork: Andrea Blum, Gardens and Plants, 2005   33 artwork: Richard Deacon, Untitled, 1980

34 Musée National d'Histoire et d'Art, Luxembourg
34–37 © Lukas Roth, www.lukas-roth.com

38 Casino Luxembourg, Forum d'art contemporain, Luxembourg
38 © Albert Biwer   40–41 © Christian Mosar   41 artwork: Peter Friedl, 10 acres and a mule, 2001

42 beaumontpublic gallery, Luxembourg
42–45 © Marco Kany, www.letoile.eu   44, 45 artworks: Su-Mei Tse, 1000 words for snow; in collaboration with Jean-Lou Majerus/Su-Mei Tse, Der Specht (the woodpecker), 1974–…; in collaboration with Jean-Lou Majerus

46 Concert Hall, Luxembourg
50–51 © Marco Kany, www.letoile.eu   46, 48–49, 51 © Jörg Hejkal

52 New National Library, Luxembourg
52 © Marco Kany, www.letoile.eu, Bolles+Wilson

54 Stade Albert Kongs, Hesperange
54–57 © Lukas Roth, www.lukas-roth.com

58 Centre National de l'Audiovisuel & Centre Culturel Régional de Dudelange, Dudelange
58, 64–65 © Roger Wagner   60–63 © CNA, Romain Girtgen

66 Cultural Centre Maison Thorn, Niederanven
66, 69 © Christof Weber

70 Rockhal II, Esch-sur-Alzette
70–72, 73 © Christof Weber   73 m. © Marco Kany, www.letoile.eu

74 Chapel, Oetrange
74–77 © Jean-Baptiste Avril

work and trade

78 Production Hall/Offices, Leudelange
78 © Marco Kany, www.letoile.eu   80–81 © Christof Weber

82 Cement Works, Esch-sur-Alzette
82, 84–85 © G. G. Kirchner

86 Production Hall with Administrative Wing, Echternach
86, 88–89 © Lukas Roth, www.lukas-roth.com

90 Jean Schmit Engineering, Luxembourg
90, 92–93 © Lukas Roth, www.lukas-roth.com

94 Office Block, Luxembourg
94 © Imedia

96 Delegation Building, Luxembourg
96, 98–99 © Willi Filz   98 © Atelier d'Architecture & de Design Jim Clemes

100 Workshops of the Administration des Ponts et Chaussées, Bertrange
100, 102–103 © Lukas Roth, www.lukas-roth.com

104 Conversion of an Industrial Building, Niederanven
104, 106–107 © Christof Weber

108 Laccolith Office Complex, Cloche d'Or
108, 110–111 © Paczowski et Fritsch Architectes

112 General Secretariat of the European Parliament, Extension and Alterations to the Konrad Adenauer Complex, Luxembourg
112, 114–115 © Heinle, Wischer und Partner Freie Architekten

116 European Court of Justice, Luxembourg
116, 118–119 © Dominique Perrault Architecture   120–121 © Marco Kany, www.letoile.eu

122 Extension for the European Court of Auditors, Luxembourg
122, 126–127 © Willi Filz   124–125 © Atelier d'Architecture & de Design Jim Clemes

128 Conference Centre, Luxembourg
128, 130–133 © Barbara Burg, Oliver Schuh, www.palladium.de

134 Heights Offices, Luxembourg
134, 137 © Raoul Somers   136 © Itten + Brechbühl AG

138 Rehazenter, Luxembourg
138, 140–145 © Christof Weber

146 SES, Betzdorf
146, 149 © Lukas Roth, www.lukas-roth.com

150 Soteg, Esch-sur-Alzette
150, 152–155 © André Weisgerber, Visions and More

banks

156 Annex for a Bank, Luxembourg
156, 159, 160–161 © Willi Filz   158 © Atelier d'Architecture & de Design Jim Clemes

162 Commerzbank Luxembourg (CISAL), Luxembourg
162, 164–165 © G. G. Kirchner

166 IKB International, Luxembourg
166, 169 © Michael Reisch

170 European Investment Bank II, Luxembourg
170, 172–173 © Ingenhoven Architekten, Düsseldorf

174 Zentralbank II, Luxembourg
174, 176–177 © Lukas Roth, www.lukas-roth.com

178 Banque Populaire, Luxembourg
178, 180–181 © Lukas Roth, www.lukas-roth.com

education

182 Pre- and Primary School, Remerschen
182, 184–185 © G. G. Kirchner

186 Foyer scolaire and École précoce-préscolaire, Hamm
186, 188–189 © Michel Feinen

190 Pre- and Pimary School, Eich-Mühlenbach
190, 192–193 © Foto-Design Waltraud Krase

194 School in Born, Mompach
194, 196–197 © igelstudios

198 Primary School, Howald
198–201 © Lukas Roth, www.lukas-roth.com

202 Sports Hall for the École primaire Dellheicht, Esch-sur-Alzette
202 © Michel Feinen   203–205 © Willi Filz

206 Extension to the Rue du Verger Primary School, Luxembourg
206, 208–209 © Marco Kany, www.letoile.eu
209 © Teisen–Giesler Architectes

210 Pre- and Primary School, Bettendorf
210–213 © Imedia

urban development

222 Ex-Industrial Site Belval, Esch-sur-Alzette
222, 225–227 © Marco Kany, www.letoile.eu

228 Station District, Luxembourg
228, 229–233 © Eddie Young

residential

234 Reconstruction of a former dairy, Bettembourg
234, 236–237 © Marco Kany, www.letoile.eu
236–237 © Gambucci Architectes

238 Social Housing, Bettembourg
238–239, 241 © Lukas Roth, www.lukas-roth.com

242 Maison Zambon, Dudelange
242, 244–245 © Lukas Roth, www.lukas-roth.com

246 Detached House, Bridel
246, 248–249 © Marco Kany, www.letoile.eu

250 Conversion of the site of the former tile factory Cerabati, Mertert-Wasserbillig
250 © Michel Feinen   250 © Willi Filz

252 Maison Lonhienne-Pierre, Peppingen
253, 254, 255 © Lukas Roth, www.lukas-roth.com

256 Youth Hostel, Echternach
256, 258–259 m. © Willi Filz 259 © Patrick Muller

260 Residential Estate Cité am Wenkel, Bertrange
260, 262–263 © Jan Kraege

264 Residential Housing, Rumelange
264–265 © Christof Weber   264 © Marco Kany, www.letoile.eu

266 Villa, Luxembourg
266, 268–269 © Marco Kany, www.letoile.eu

270 Renovation of an Old Town Quarter, Luxembourg
270 © Fonds de Rénovation de la Vieille Ville   272–273 © Imedia
273 © Arlette Schneiders Architectes

274 Villa De Meyer-Fasbender, Villa Freising, Luxembourg
274, 276 © Christof Weber   274, 277 © Andrés Lejona

278 Moko House, Schuttrange
278, 280–281 © Lukas Roth, www.lukas-roth.com

282 Avalon, Luxembourg/Kirchberg
282, 284 © G. G. Kirchner   284–285 © Marianne Brausch, Fonds Kirchberg   285 © Michel Feinen

gardens and parks

286 Garden of the Banque de Luxembourg, Luxembourg
286, 288–289 © Marco Kany, www.letoile.eu

290 Parc Jacquinot, Bettembourg
290 © Lukas Roth, www.lukas-roth.com

pavilions

292 Arcelor, Esch-sur-Alzette
292–293 © Marco Kany, www.letoile.eu

294 Economie, Esch-sur-Alzette
294 © Marco Kany, www.letoile.eu   295 © Steve Troes

296 Skip, Esch-sur-Alzette
296–297 © Marco Kany, www.letoile.eu

298 Pavilion, Heinerscheid; Light Bar, Luxembourg
298 © Christof Weber   298 © n-lab architects

infrastructure

300 Terminal A at Luxembourg Airport
300, 302–303 © Paczowski et Fritsch Architectes

306 Block-Type Thermal Power Station Kirchberg, Luxembourg
306, 308–311 © Lukas Roth, www.lukas-roth.com

312 Radar Tower, Luxembourg-Findel
312 © Lukas Roth, www.lukas-roth.com

314 Reservoir, Hivange
314 © Georges Reuter Architectes s.à.r.l.

316 Route du Nord, Viaduc de Lorentzweiler
316–317 © Willi Filz

318 Reservoir / Technical Service and Fire Department, Leudelange
318, 320–321 © Barbara Burg, Oliver Schuh, www.palladium.de

patrimony

322 Emile Mayrisch Monument, Esch-sur-Alzette
322–323 © Marco Kany, www.letoile.eu

324 The Red Bridge, Luxembourg
324, 330–331 © Marco Kany, www.letoile.eu
326–329 © Cosanti Foundation

reflection

334 constructive, Emmanuel J. Petit
334 © akg-images / Erich Lessing   337 © Ulf Meyer
338, 341 © Philipp Meuser

Plans and animations by courtesy of the respective architects

This project is kindly supported by

AGNES FRANCOIS ET JEAN S.à r.l.

BAATZ CONSTRUCTIONS S.à r.l.

BALTHASAR CONSTRUCTIONS S.à r.l.
www.balthasar.lu

BARTZ CONSTRUCTIONS S.à r.l.
www.bartz.lu

BONARIA ET FILS S.à r.l.
www.bonaria.lu

BONARIA FRERES S.A.
www.bonaria-freres.lu

C. KARP-KNEIP CONSTRUCTIONS S.A
www.karpkneip.lu

CDC COMPAGNIE DE CONSTRUCTION
S.à r.l. & Cie Secs
www.cdclu.lu

CLOOS S.A.
www.cloos.lu

COMPAGNIE LUXEMBOURGEOISE D'ENTREPRISES S.A. - C.L.E.
www.cle.lu

COSTANTINI S.A.
www.costantini.lu

DELLI ZOTTI S.A.
www.dellizotti.lu

E . G . C . S.à r.l.

ENTREPRISE DE CONSTRUCTIONS CLAUDE JANS S.A.
www.cjans.lu

ENTREPRISE DE TRAVAUX EUROPEENS S.A.
www.edte.lu

Entreprise **GREIVELDINGER** S.à r.l.

Entreprise **JULES FARENZENA** S.à r.l.
www.farenzena.lu

Entreprise **POECKES** S.à r.l.

Entreprise **THEO VINANDY**

ETS. KUHN S.A.
www.kuhn-construction.lu

FELIX GIORGETTI S.à r.l.
www.gio.lu

HT-LUX S.A.
www.hochtief.lu

I.L.C.O. S.à r.l.
www.ilco.lu

J.P. RINNEN & FILS S.à r.l.
www.rinnen.lu

JOS. BALTHASAR S.à r.l.

JULIEN CAJOT & CIE S.e.c.s.
www.jcajot.lu

KISCH S.A.
www.kisch.lu

KURT CONSTRUCTIONS S.A.
www.kurt.lu

LUX T.P. S.A.

NIC. SCHILLING & FILS S.à r.l.
www.schilling.lu

OBG-LUX S.A.
www.obg-lux.lu

PERRARD S.à r.l.
www.perrard.lu

RECYMA S.A.
www.recyma.lu

SCHOLTES & BRAUCH S.A.
www.scholtes-brauch.lu

S. L. CHANZY-PARDOUX S.à r.l. (S.L.C.P.)

SOGEROUTE S.à r.l.
www.sogeroute.lu

SOLUDEC S.A.
www.soludec.com

SOTRAP S.à r.l.
www.sotrap.lu

STUGALUX CONSTRUCTION S.A.
www.stugalux.lu

T-COMALUX S.A.

TRACOL S.A.
www.tracol.lu

TRAGEC S.à r.l.

TRAGELUX S.A.
www.tragelux.lu

TRALUX S.à r.l.
www.tralux.lu

WICKLER FRERES EXPLOITATION S.à r.l.
www.wickler.lu

GROUPEMENT DES ENTREPRENEURS ASBL   L-1013 Luxembourg   T. (00352) 43 60 24   F. (00352) 43 23 28

Partners of the Fondation de l'Architecture et de l'Ingénierie Luxembourg

BANQUE DE LUXEMBOURG

 ANNEN   BUROtrend

 CEGEDEL   CIMALUX

 HOCHTIEF LUXEMBOURG HT LUX   C. KARP-KNEIP

 IKOGEST   Luxcontrol

 PAUL WURTH   Prefalux

a+p kieffer omnitec

Kindly supported by
Ministère de la Culture et de l'Enseignement Supérieur et de la Recherche / Ordre des Architectes et des Ingénieurs – Conseils et du Fonds Culturel National

**LX architecture – in the heart of europe
contemporary architecture in luxembourg**

Edited by
Fondation de l'Architecture et de l'Ingénierie, Luxembourg

ISBN 978-3-938666-69-2

© 2008 DOM publishers
www.dom-publishers.com

© Layout and design: Vidale-Gloesener
www.vidalegloesener.lu

Editors
Cornelia Dörries, Uta Keil

Translation
Amanda Crain, Dresden
Cord von der Lühe, Berlin
Paul Skidmore, Berlin

Picture editor
Marco Kany, www.letoile.eu

The *Deutsche Bibliothek* lists this publication in the *Deutsche Nationalbibliografie*; detailed bibliographic data is available on the internet at http://dnb.ddb.de

This work is subject to copyright. All rights are reserved, whether the whole or part of the material is concerned, specifically the rights of translation, reprinting, recitation, broadcasting, reproduction on microfilms or in other ways, and storage or processing in data bases.

All photos and drawings by courtesy of the respective firms, architects and photographers. Sources and owners of rights are stated to the best of our knowledge; please signal any we have might omitted.

DOM publishers